Repatriated

Repatriated

A Novel in Sixty Scenes

ADRIAAN VAN DIS

Translated from the Dutch by David Colmer

WILLIAM HEINEMANN: LONDON

Published by William Heinemann, 2008

2 4 6 8 10 9 7 5 3 1

Copyright © Adriaan van Dis, 2002

English translation © David Colmer 2007

Adriaan Van Dis has asserted his right under the Copyright, Designs
and Patents Act 1988 to be identified as the author of this work

First published in the Netherlands in 2002, in Dutch under the title
Familieziek, by Augustus, part of the Contact Group, Amsterdam

William Heinemann
Random House, 20 Vauxhall Bridge Road,
London SW1V 2SA

www.randomhouse.co.uk

Addresses for companies within The Random House Group Limited
can be found at:
www.randomhouse.co.uk

The Random House Group Limited Reg. No. 954009

A CIP catalogue record for this book
is available from the British Library

ISBN: 9780434011803

Mixed Sources

Product group from well-managed
forests and other controlled sources
www.fsc.org Cert no. TT-COC-2139
© 1996 Forest Stewardship Council

FSC

Typeset by Palimpsest Book Production Limited, Grangemouth, Stirlingshire
Printed and bound in Great Britain by
CPI Mackays, Chatham ME5 8TD

Contents

one more time

'One more time and I'm packing my bags,' Mother says, storming out of the sitting room. In the hall she changes her mind, there's no time like the present. 'I'm going now!' she screams. 'You hear me, *now*!' She slams the doors, makes a racket pulling a suitcase out from under the bed, opens the rusty locks, drums out the dust – a button falls to the floor, along with a few yellowed menus. The wardrobe swings open . . . there go her blouses, dresses, skirts, vests, cardigans, nylons, socks, her stole . . . She's packing for winter and summer. And taking the papers too, her secret bankbook. She's packing for good.

Cautiously the girls creep into the bedroom, positioning themselves between suitcase and wardrobe. Mother doesn't even put down what she's holding to push them out of the way . . . Hat. A silver hairbrush. Hairdressing cape. The bottle of Soir de Paris. She piles it up. The eldest locks the door and pockets the key. 'What about us?' she asks. Mother counts her hankies. As fast as she can fold and pack, the girls put it all back on the bed next to the suitcase. They rummage through her clothes and sprinkle each other with Soir de Paris, the hat goes from head to head.

'What's *brandade*?' asks the eldest, who has picked the menus up off the floor.

'Stockfish, we ate that in Genoa.'

'And *scaloppine*?'

'Shellfish, I think . . . wasn't that Naples?'

'Yuck,' shouts the youngest.

Mother sits down on the edge of the bed, the anger draining from her face as she savours an old voyage: '. . . camel meat in Aden, king crab in Singapore . . .'

'When do we get to go on a boat again?' asks the middle daughter.

'Sweetheart, it's much too expensive now.'

The oldest waves the bankbook in the air.

'Put that down, that's for us . . . for later.' She grabs at the bankbook. 'For God's sake don't mention it . . . don't tell him about it, ever.'

'So you're taking us with you?'

Mother pulls her youngest closer. 'How could I ever leave you?' The other two throw themselves on to the bed as well. They roll into the middle of the mattress – Mother bobbing between her daughters – and throw their arms around each other, kissing and cuddling. They brush each other's hair with the silver brush. The eldest wraps the stole around Mother's shoulders, the youngest puts on the hairdressing cape. They used to lie around like this in the old days too; under a quiet, humming fan at all those strange outposts and later, in the clammy heat of war, on a mat on the floor. An island of women. They creep even closer together, stroking their mother. If only it could stay like this for ever. Hugging and tickling.

Mother stretches and picks her daughter's pocket for the key. 'Don't worry,' she sighs. She'll try one more time, pretend nothing's happened. Come on . . . get up, put the kettle on and make a sandwich for the angry man standing at the window in the sitting room. But the girls pull her back down on the bed and hold her tight. They imitate his *satay* accent and joke about his bandy legs and his clothes, the trousers with the bum seam stretched to bursting. From all that sitting.

'Too lazy to work,' says the eldest.

'You chose him,' says Mother.

'Yeah, back then . . .'

'Because *you* said we needed a father,' says the middle one.

'But not a little brother,' says the youngest.

'Who's completely different . . .'

3

'Not one of us . . .'

'No, if he was he'd be better looking.' The girls laugh and all talk at once. 'That nose . . . Yes, that nose!' They crack up. 'And those legs . . . no . . . yes, he's got them too! He's starting to look more and more like his father.'

'Stop it.' Mother smothers her voice in her daughters' laps and wipes her tears off on their stomachs; her hands dig through the clothes spread out over the bed, she lifts the stole up to her face to stroke her cheeks and eyelids . . . Remembering the old softness.

She takes a deep breath, brushes away her sadness and opens the bedroom door. A pair of boy's legs scurry round the corner into the bathroom. She walks into the hall and stops in front of the bathroom door. 'I'm only doing it for you, remember that,' she says to whoever's listening.

shoeshine

'So, Cleaner,' Mother asks, 'what's it today: hall, stable or shoes?'

He wouldn't turn his nose up at some shoes, but which ones?

'His, of course.'

'The black ones, the brown ones, the boots, the brogues?'

'All of them.'

His lordship has ten pairs. Ten of the best. Hard-wearing. Twenty noses begging for a buffing. Shoes for good weather, shoes for bad weather, dignified shoes, climbing shoes, hiking boots. A pair for riding and a pair for dancing. The dance shoes are the most beautiful. Soft, gleaming black. When Cleaner presses the soles with his thumbs, they curl in his hands. Mr Java is a dancer who lifts women up and swirls them round the room: lightly near the record-player – the needle would bounce out of the groove – wildly at the back of the room . . . through the door, down

5

the hall, into every corner of the house. Glenn Miller gets you going.

With the dance shoe in his hand the boy hears the trumpet . . . Mother and the girls are ready, standing hip to hip. No, he can't squeeze in between, dancing is for women. Mother smiles as her husband takes her in his arms, one turn and her slip is showing, a hairpin comes loose, her locks and wrinkles are dancing. The three girls follow her with their eyes, arms interlocked, skirts swinging to the rhythm. Still dancing, Mr Java leads Mother to a chair, first sister leaps forward – pressing against Mr Java, cheek to cheek. Middle sister steps into his outstretched arms, just two turns around the floor, she'd rather read a book. He bows for third sister, lifting her up and swinging her round, showing the whole room her knickers. And then Cleaner gets a shot after all, to finish off, with his sweaty socks on the polished noses, hitching a ride to the rhythm. Mr Java pulls back his toes, tickling him under his feet – for a second, Cleaner is standing on a ridge of bone – then he lowers them again and lets him slide softly over his toes . . .

—

The boy applies polish to the dance shoes enthusi-astically, he even does the soles. But aren't the other nine pairs overdoing it? Everyone is scandalised – aunts, great uncles, Grandfather, neighbours: 'How does he do it?' 'No job, but still he shops at Bally.'

'Your father's got a hole in his pocket.' Mother says: 'we turn our collars, we wear each other's hand-me-downs, we cut our coat according to our cloth and he plays the big shot.' To prove it, she opens a wardrobe and runs her fingers over his shirts, 'Six, eight, twelve, sixteen, twenty-four . . . that should get him through at least two more wars.' She jerks another door open, the trouser hangers click against each other in fright, coats swing shoulder to shoulder and pass the word: Dear, dear, dear! Overdone! Coats for all seasons. And ties! Stripes, dots, tartan . . . and cufflinks: muffled tinkling inside a velvet box.

'He's a dandy,' says middle sister.

'He can't accept it's over,' says Mother.

'Incorrigible,' says first sister.

———

His lordship has to adjust. From country homes to the home country. He has to face facts, that's what the girls say and they got it from Mother. But the facts don't seem to make any impression – listen to what he's done now: while everyone else in the house scrimps and saves, he's gone and bought yet another pair of shoes. Ten obviously weren't enough! His new acquisitions are sitting on the table brazenly: black loafers with shiny buckles. So you can swing with no strings attached – the old pair weren't suitable for jazz and jive. Real calfskin . . . for the girls that might be the worst of all. They came with two yellow flannel bags and a cedar shoe-tree in each shoe – that alone must have cost a fortune. And whose money did he use? It was the housekeeping money, Mother's money. An outrage, say the girls, who have grown up thrifty: not throwing anything out, unpicking old cardigans and knitting socks from the wool, and when the socks get holes in them, darning them. They grow into hand-me-downs. You fix shoes, even when a toe is peeking out: you patch your shoe and walk around with a pretty leather plaster. That's how *they* go to school!

Mr Java says, 'The more you have, the less you wear out.' He holds up the gleaming soles. A coat of arms is branded on the bottom. Only kings dance in shoes like these.

'Couldn't you wait?' asks Mother.

'They look more expensive than they were,' he says.

'We need a new boiler before winter.'

It keeps Mother awake at night. The girls have seen him stroking his new shoes. 'My God, I ask you, what kind of man strokes a shoe?'

The shoes keep nagging until Mother gets them out of their bags and greases them, with saddle grease – very measured, but still it has the whole house snickering. She scowls as she puts the loafers back in the yellow bags and ties a double knot in the drawstrings.

Into the cabin trunk with them, and the key goes into the secret drawer in the bureau. The shoes can hardly breathe. 'That will keep the leather supple,' she says, 'we'll postpone their dance for a few years.'

The girls understand. 'We have to protect him from himself.'

For the time being Glenn Miller stays in his cover.

behind the curtain 1

The girls gather in the bicycle hall, behind the curtain.
The boy follows their feet and listens in.

'It can't go on like this.'

'He's driving Mummy mad.'

'We'd be better off without him.'

'A ridiculous man.'

'He only costs us money.'

'He's got to go.'

'He was a pig in a poke.'

Horse-Man

Mr Java speaks the language of horses, his voice makes their ears tremble. Even farmers' nags understand him. The leather saddle was more familiar than his mother's lap, he learnt to walk between horses in the stable. His father owned a stud that catered to court and cavalry. (That was then, in the old days, before the war, overseas, in the country he prefers to leave unnamed – the land of his birth.) It made them a fortune . . . The horse that laid the golden egg. Look at the photo albums: plantations, racetrack, country homes with whitewashed verandas and starched servants, a cream-coloured Hispano-Suiza . . . all gone now, ravaged by war and rebellion. Since the voyage he's tried not to look back. Only the weak get homesick.

Horses eat out of the palm of his hand in the new country too. When he's at home standing at the window – and he does that every day, looking out is his profession – he sees their brown backs gleaming through the pines across the road. The paddock is by the wood. It's a field of longing, but they're unrid-able. They're rag-and-bone horses – old, gaunt and sagging, skittish from being tormented on the streets, they hardly let strangers pat them. But he picks roadside clover for them and blows gently into their nostrils. They lick his fingers in gratitude and, after a few feeding sessions, even the most timid nag stretches its neck out, begging for a hand to tousle its mane. He keeps their spirits up, because their paddock is the abattoir's waiting room: as soon as there's some flesh on their bones, they'll be turned into smoked sausage.

But they're not the only horses in the village. There are strong, healthy animals in a large stable behind the dunes, close to the beach. They don't play, they are ready for action: they are the lifeboat horses. Zeeland draught horses, heavy, with hoofs like buoys, manes of rope, and legs that are stronger than oars – they pull the lifeboats straight into the breakers, muscles tight as cables. As soon as the crew can row out to the ship in distress under their own steam, the horses swim back to shore: manes dancing like ruffs and tails trimmed with froth. The sight makes Mr Java tremble with happiness.

When the alarm sounds, he tries to rout the whole family from bed, sometimes in the middle of the night, arm in arm to the beach. After all these years Mother and the girls can't be bothered, but he still drags the boy along.

The boy can't stand the smell of horses, but does his best to love them, especially since the town council appointed Mr Java to exercise them. The animals just stand there getting stiff in their stable, waiting for shipwrecks that hardly ever happen, and nowadays, when the alarm does sound, they often have to stay inside anyway because the neighbouring villages up and down the coast have traded their horses for tractors and can turn out much faster. The idea was Mr Java's, he must have dedicated at least twenty letters to it, and at last the mayor has come round: Mr Java may now officially call himself the Horse Exercise Master. Recognition – even if he doesn't get a cent for it. Because, as the mayor informed him in writing, it's a favour.

'Horse-Man,' the girls sometimes call Mr Java behind his back. He knows: it's a name he's proud of.

—

Mr Java's boyhood dream is within reach again: a stable of his own. Eight head-shaking horses he can take out riding. He encourages cumbersome cart-horses into a sublime canter; under his legs the Zeeland draught horses trot in another country, not through the clay where the plough has made their chests broad and their hoofs heavy, but on lofty paths between tea plantations. Best of all is riding them at ebb over a wet glistening beach, where the water reflects the clouds as mountains he can gallop straight through. Splashing his paradise to pieces. Because only the weak get homesick.

And to think that his only child is allergic to horses. The boy turns red the moment he gets close to a horse. How is that possible with a lineage like his? Farmers on one side and horsemen on the other, generation after generation, and then suddenly this delicate shoot . . . even though he and his wife took everything they could get their hands on to bring an able-bodied child into the world.

The boy sees things differently. The other day, when he had to sweep out the stable by himself, he gave one of the nags a terrible whack with the broom, because he panicked. Or was it out of viciousness? The animal couldn't walk for a week. It's not the boy who's scared of the horses: the horses are scared of him.

Horse-Man doesn't know that.

antibodies

The first signals came within a month of the atomic tests. Mother picked them up: the news had just finished, the radio dance band was playing its theme tune and suddenly she heard a strange ruffle . . . Morse code, she thought, a signal from a planet in distress. Mr Java said she was just imagining things: she didn't sleep well, when that happens you tend to hear strange noises. He didn't sleep well either. None of them did. To reassure her, the girls went outside for a look but the noise had long been swallowed by the wind in the pines. They turned off the radio and a strange silence crept through the house. The next evening the ruffle came back. Mr Java refused to hear it. And it had been like that for days. Tonight the family is sitting around the radio again. But it's not working. The dial glides mutely past the stations. Even the Voice of America is silent. But still they hear the ruffling. It's not coming from the radio after all.

The geraniums shiver on the windowsill. After a few weird warm days, a cold snap has suddenly arrived and the weather strips are shrinking in the cracks.

A vicious east wind is sweeping across the country, the newspaper predicts Siberian conditions. Strange geese from the taiga have settled in the catchment area, but Mother has also seen a lark flying back and forth with twigs in its beak. Nature proves the point she has been making for days: the climate is all mixed up.

The boy has found monstrous jellyfish washed up on the beach. Too tough to chop into pieces. He saw warships sailing past. The day before that, he heard jet fighters above the clouds. He doesn't dare to mention it at home; near the radio he has to hold his tongue – even when they are listening to silence.

'It was close this time,' Mother says, as Mr Java turns his back to assume his position in front of the window, feet apart, hands in pockets. 'Are any windows open?'

'In weather like this?'

'Is the stable door shut?'

'I checked there just before dinner.' She could have known, his coat still smelt of straw.

'Shouldn't you . . .'

'I bolted it,' he snaps. He's not paying attention, he's angry with the radio.

'I have a strange feeling,' says Mother. 'Who's going?'

Not the girls, they did the dishes. 'It's men's work,'

they say. Mr Java massages the muscles around his heart – he's too exhausted. Mother stands up, walks to the hall and gets the stable key down from the hook. The girls nod at the boy. The boy looks at the dark windows. The stable is behind the big dune, at least five minutes' walk from the house. It's pitch-black outside, moon and stars are hidden.

'Hey, someone asked you a question.'

He doesn't hear who's speaking, the strange ruffling noise is still in his ears, but he knows what's expected of him. All eyes are pointing at him, firing bolts at his head, making his cheeks glow. 'Hey, you there.'

At home they call him kid, lad or boy, or after the chore he has to do: cleaner, duster, sweeper. And some-times, when the girls are cuddling up to him, they call him brother, very sweetly. They never use his name. And that's just as well, because he can't stand it. He wishes he had a different name every day.

'Here,' says Mother, throwing the key at the boy, who has to duck to avoid getting hit on the head, 'it's your turn.'

'But then I'll be sneezing all night again.'

'And bring me back a horsehair.'

'*Yeuch.*' The boy makes gagging noises. 'What for?'

'As proof you've been in the stable.'

17

The boy pulls on his coat and boots, looks for a full hurricane lantern in the hall and grabs the axe. The wind is fresh and biting, the lantern doesn't go out. He doesn't sneeze, he's not short of breath, and he has his weapon: a heavy axe that feels ice-cold on his fingers, good for chopping necks and stampeding horses and Russians and Martians and watchful geese. He sniffs at the metal to calm his nose. He's not the one who's afraid, it's his nose that gets scared, sometimes, of horsehair, dust . . . atoms from Siberia. The axe calms him down. He holds his breath a few times to listen properly, once for each sound: the waves, the sea in the pines, the wind in the marram grass, his boots slapping against his calves. From behind the dune he suddenly hears the ruffling again – loud and wooden. He hits the ground, holds the axe tight and listens, twisting his neck to search the sky . . . The flying saucers and rockets stay out of sight. Dung fills the air: the stench of horse hanging in this hollow in the lee of the dunes. His eyes are watering, the muscles in his neck are throbbing, a sneezing fit is on its way. He tries to swallow the irritation. The ruffling must be the horses, restless hoofs on wooden panels.

The boy holds the lantern high and crawls to the stable. He inspects the lock: shut, untouched. And inside there's the ruffling. His axe rattles against the stable's tarred planks; the horses whinny. The boy talks to the stable door the way he's heard Mr Java do many times, 'It's just me.' The ruffling stops. Then he talks to his axe, blows out his fear and sucks air in until his lungs are full to bursting. The door handle feels dry in his hand.

Quickly: the lantern on the hook, the axe on the ground, to the first box . . . his breath pounding in his ribs. The horse recoils. Stroke horse, good horse – two pats on the neck. His eyes are watering – without looking he pulls a hair out of the mane. The horse snorts, scrapes a hoof through the straw. He's got the lantern and axe again. Into the cold air, clean out those lungs. Dribble running down on to his coat. But he has a prize haul in his hand, he hasn't torn out one hair but a whole tuft. Into his pocket with it, far from his nose. Axe poised, lantern raised and home. The iron glitters, the axe lifts him up, he flies along behind it. The knight has fulfilled his quest.

Mr Java is a black silhouette in front of the window. The girls pretend to read, Mother sits under the stand-ard lamp with needle and thread, the boy's pyjamas on her lap. As if there was never any danger. 'It was just the horses,' the boy says.

'Spooked by the mice, maybe,' suggests first sister. The girls sigh with relief. But Mr Java curses under his breath. 'They feel something, animals know more than we do.'

Mother holds out a hand, a silent hand demanding proof. The boy hands her the tuft of hair. She picks out the longest and wraps it around the top button of his pyjama jacket. 'If you sleep with this, you'll build up antibodies,' she says. 'You have to beat it.'

Mother is not afraid, never has been. She's not just smart, she's also the most sensible woman he knows. A mother like her will get you through the war. Even if he suffocates that night in his bed, she loves him.

headpower

Mr Java is standing at the window with his hands in his pockets, looking dark and dangerous. He's listening to the radio news service. He isn't glad that the radio is working again, he's furious: his ears are trembling, his hands swell into fists and the bum seam of his trousers is about to burst. He's raging, Mr Java, and he swears at the news-reader. 'What does that buffoon know about it? Collective security ... Before you know it they'll be pounding on the door here too. Blathering idiots. Soft-headed pacifists.' His son is sitting behind him, at the dining table, with his drawing box open and his hands resting on a big sheet of white paper. He draws a giant at a misty window, black on grey, and a windowsill with geraniums left and right. He draws a radio to go with it – a square on legs. The square is vomiting a balloon, a balloon for words, but empty, even if the boy knows exactly what goes inside it. He knows the tirades off by heart, he hears them every day . . . he just doesn't dare to write them down.

'It'll soon be time to pack and go again,' says Mr Java. 'But where?' He silences the radio and turns to face the boy. 'Away, away,' he growls, dragging the words through the room. He creeps up to the table, pretending an enemy's after him.

A shot! The boy jumps.

Mr Java has slammed the drawing box shut with one finger on the lid. 'Before you know it, they've got you, like a pencil in a box.' He rattles the box loudly next to the boy's ear.

'Don't,' the boy shouts, 'the points . . .'

'Listen to them moan,' says Mr Java. 'They can't colour or shade now . . . or write . . . they're stuck in the dark and can't speak . . . that could happen to you.'

It's all because of the news. News that has to be turned off when Mother is in the room. But today she's gone to the city with the girls, so Mr Java is listening every hour. 'If they take you prisoner, remember one thing: don't break.' He slides his chair up to the boy and whispers, 'Be like a reed: bend, lie flat in the storm, make yourself small if you have to, but stand up again. Think of something else and make yourself invulnerable . . . Headpower, that's what it comes down to, headpower is the best defence. Yogis have it, fakirs . . . Up in the Himalayas there are yogis who sit in front of a cave and melt the snow around them; a practised fakir can lie down on a bed of nails. In time you should be able to too . . .'

The boy looks at him with frightened disbelief.

'I'll teach you . . . It's an ancient art. Headpower dispels hunger and pain. Headpower keeps you going, no matter where you are . . . in a cattle car, in prison, a torture chamber or a Siberian work camp.' Mr Java grins, opens the drawing box and makes a pencil dance on one finger. A pencil with a crooked yellow point. 'Headpower lets you see colours and smell sunflowers, even if it's pitch-black around you.'

It helped Mr Java a lot, in the old days. An old man had taught him, and that old man had learnt it from an Indian: passing on the art was a duty . . . 'Strange, it's all coming back to me.' He could kick himself, but he settles for hitting himself, on the forehead — with the palm of his hand.

You know what it takes? Your head, that's all. Dreams, wishes, memories, that weird nose of yours . . . you use all your senses to get your brains going.

Rules? There are none. Although . . . you have to practise, like you do with everything else in life.

'Think about a colour,' Mr Java says.

The boy slides his drawing paper aside.

'Have you got one?'

He nods.

'Has something come to mind?'

Another nod.

'Think about it hard, very hard . . .'

The boy thinks visibly, screwing up his eyes.

'And?' Mr Java begs. 'Have your thoughts started travelling?'

No, the boy shakes his head fiercely, no.

'Impossible! They have to, it's automatic. What do you see before you?'

'You.'

'Me? What an honour! I didn't realise I was a colour.'

The boy looks at his drawing out of the corner of his eye.

'Or do you mean this suit?' Mr Java runs his hand over the fabric. 'Harris tweed. Moss . . . er . . . palm green. Come on, what do you think of when you see this?'

'You?' says the bewildered boy.

A sigh, a deep sigh. Mr Java storms out of the room.

But in the boy's head, Mr Java doesn't take a step, he stays standing where he was standing, in front of the window with his hands in his pockets. Black against the light from outside. He has stood there for as long as he can remember. From early in the morning until late in the afternoon. A tweed statue, listening to the same old news.

—

Alone at the table, bent over his drawing paper and listening to Mr Java's footsteps in the hall, the boy thinks of his cot, for no reason, without trying to, as if an invisible hand has led him to the bedroom. A cot he grew out of years ago. The smell of the mattress rises up within him: eelgrass and the piss of poor children. The sound too, footsteps on frozen moss. He's not allowed to say it stinks. He should be grateful for the cot: it was donated and donating is a more noble form of giving. So many things in the house were donated. The family is cloaked in gratitude. The bars of the cot are loose, they squeak when you turn them – if you strum the whole row you can play guitar. He lies on his stomach with his head at the foot, under the blankets. He's looking for something. It's dark . . . he can't find his way out. He's almost suffocating . . . The memory stalls . . . Black. Bars . . . That's all, no matter how hard he sniffs.

Is this what Mr Java means?

The boy keeps the memory to himself.

ear tears

Mr Java cleans his ears, in front of the window. With the nails of his little fingers first, to loosen the wax, then with a hairpin to scratch the passageways clean. When the bend is full, he inspects the colour, humming with satisfaction at the thread of dark yellow before wiping his catch onto his hankie. 'Wax is hearing's first line of defence,' he says. That's what you get from listening to the news every hour. What's more, the wax production of the ear increases in cold countries. You need to know things like that.

Mr Java holds up his hankie: ear tears. 'My ears are weeping . . . begging for other sounds. Not news, but birds. The birds from the old days. What kind of noises are there to hear at night here? Do you ever lie terrified in bed? Does a tiger ever rustle through the undergrowth, does a snake ever hiss on the veranda?'

'The sea,' the boy says.

'The sea . . . yes, that is beautiful . . .' says Mr Java. 'But what a miserable colour.'

Mr Java sits down. Snap, says the back seam of his trousers. 'There are no decent tailors here either,' he grumbles stoically.

the photo album

Mr Java opens his photo album. It's only about an inch thick but he can still get totally lost in its panoramic valleys, botanical gardens, broad rivers and volcanic craters. He lost all his photos during the war. Later, sisters and distant aunts made that loss good by sending him all kinds of photos from their own albums. Now he can show his boy how rubber grows, and coffee and tea, and how the natives set fish traps. No, he's not homesick, only the weak get homesick. He just wants to explain things, to teach the boy something. Look and learn. He spells out the names of flora and fauna – the more exotic the better – and draws fruit, seeds, strange fins and bizarre beaks. The boy wishes he could remember it all, but he turns the words back to front and says the letters the wrong way round and when something does stick in his mind, he stresses the wrong syllable and the whole family laughs at him. That's why he looks on in silence, meekly following his guide's yellow index finger. He does feel a leech on his leg when Mr Java tells him how he had to wade through the mangrove swamps, and he really does hear the surf against the bottom of the outrigger proa – headpower, he's getting the hang of it. And when he sees the dressed-up people gathered on docks and railway station platforms or visiting the governor, he's glad he doesn't have to clean their white shoes.

Leafing through the album, Mr Java forgets his 'illustrative education' (that's what he calls it, as a permanent excuse to pick up the album with his boy). His finger lingers longer and longer on the people – not on himself, although he's in almost every photo, in his white suit, jodhpurs or uniform. He greets the men in the photos . . . Almost all dead. Since the peace – 'armed peace', according to Mr Java – his family is made up mostly of widows. But the album keeps them all alive. The dead walk the earth, stable their horses, slide chairs up to tables on the veranda and raise glasses . . . They listen to music and postpone the war. When Mr Java turns a page, the boy hears the rustling of the ladies' long skirts . . . The old days were yesterday, at least twice a week. So he can learn something.

Besides being a horseman, Mr Java turns out to be a lady's man as well, because in his album the ladies clearly have the upper hand. They too have names. All of them. Both young and old. The boy can't get over how fast people grow in photos. Faster than rubber, coffee and tea. Cousins climb from their mothers' laps on to horses' backs and schoolgirls grow busts in a single page. They dress up as tennis players, rally drivers, equestrians – especially equestrians – side saddle in long skirts or sporty and straddling the horses in breeches. Helped up by a young Java, or sliding from the saddle into his arms. Captured in sepia snapshots, each and every one remarkably blonde and named in white ink, kept young for ever between the album's cobweb pages.

'They're tough,' Mr Java says. That alone is reason enough to respect women in the tropics.

'The girls too?' asks the boy.

'The girls most of all, they saved their mother.'

The boy knows the stories. His sisters were heroines during the war. Mothers to their mother. When she was bedridden and swollen from malnutrition, they went out scavenging for food. And Mr Java owes his life to a woman too . . . He says it in a dreamy voice, but the boy wakes up and straightens his back. 'Is she in the album?' he asks eagerly.

'By then people had long stopped taking photos.'

'During the war?'

'No, afterwards . . .' The boy has to draw the words out of him. 'During the uprising . . . She was special . . . strong, intelligent.' When he was wounded, she took him to a safe hiding place – and she could see very well in the dark.

'What was she called?'

'Blue Girl.'

The boy looks at him in surprise. 'Funny name.'

'Not for a horse,' says Mr Java. 'She was a dark, beautiful Seglawi . . .' Shocked by his own answer – as if caught out – he gets a grip on himself, 'Um . . . a woman gave her to me.'

Women, they get you through.

—

Mr Java slams the photo album shut. The old days are over.

'I want to go to the Indies too,' says the boy.

'No, that's impossible now, for ever.' And anyway, he doesn't want to hear that name in a young mouth. It's not called that any more in the atlas, or on the globe table lamp he gave the boy for his birthday.

Mr Java doesn't actually want to talk about those days any more – looking is enough, the photos speak for themselves. It's the lessons that matter. And this time he's shown his boy how to help women mount a horse, how to slide a chair up to a dining table, and that you should remain standing until all the ladies are seated. Being courteous to women, that is what the album's taught him today. Colonial manners.

—

Things he should never forget: arrange bearers when the river has burst its banks and, when a lady is being

31

lifted up, never look under her skirts. On a gangplank, the man goes first, so that he can offer the woman a helping hand half-way. It is an honour to carry her tennis racket or groom her horse. Help her in and out of the car and, if it's a convertible, wrap her up against the wind. And when she's going out, help her with the buttons at the back. Without pulling any faces.

The boy nods seriously, determined . . . But at home, what's he supposed to do at home? No car, no river for miles around, a tame sea that stays behind the dunes. The only tennis, table tennis. At home they never dine, they *eat* and no one ever slides a chair up to the table for a lady. The photos puff Mr Java up, he deludes himself about how distinguished he is – until he explodes – because the boy knows all too well what happens at dinnertime: one misplaced word, any giggling, or a serviette that accidentally falls to the floor and the gravy boat smashes against the wall. Just like that. Launched by a slight tremble in Mr Java's hand. And even if he says 'sorry' ten times afterwards, it's Mother who slides back her chair to assess the damage on the floor, and it's the girls who get down on their knees to brush the pieces into the dustpan and the boy who pats the wallpaper ('Don't rub, you'll rub holes in it') very, very carefully, with lukewarm suds . . . and fails to remove the greasy stain. The dinette gets wallpapered four times a year.

And if Mother is lugging a heavy bag back from the village, Mr Java stands at the window with his hands in his pockets – doesn't even notice her. For himself, the boy likes to lie on the floor to enjoy the view when the girls step over him. That's what it's like at their house, behind closed doors.

And outside, on the streets? Do the people outside have colonial manners? In summer on the beach you hear men scolding their wives and you see boys splashing girls. Some women smoke on the boulevard – another thing Mr Java is fiercely opposed to – and others apply lipstick in public . . . even worse. Sometimes you see a butt with a red kiss in the gutter: double indecorum.

'The third-class manners,' says Mr Java, 'of the rancid-flannel tribe.'

That's a tribe you never see in the photos from the old days.

writing lesson

Mr Java looks at the clock. Five past nine. The radio valves are still humming, the news has just finished, he listened to it with Mother. For the first time in ages. He was restrained, the way she wants him to be, and even if he couldn't help swearing under his breath, he looked calm: the valerian drops seem to be helping. Mother left the room with a smile on her face, then raced off to her sewing lesson on her bike.

Mr Java is spending his time just as profitably. Every morning he gives his boy home education, six days a week, whenever his health allows – reading, writing, arithmetic and geography, plus lessons for life of course. The time for learning through play is long past.

What's keeping that kid anyway? He heard him just a minute ago. He knows he has to be on time, the news is his school bell. Mr Java taps his watch, pulls up a chair and sits down at the big table. His right shoe feels an arm, a back, a leg . . . The shoe kicks. Above the table the hands don't betray a thing, they straighten a stack of white sheets. Straighter than straight, next to a fountain pen, a pencil, a rubber, an exercise book and a pencil sharpener. The tools of the teacher.

'I was first!' shouts the boy, crawling out from under the table.

'Today I'm going to teach you something special,' Mr Java says. 'We're going to join the letters up together. Enough of that clumsy block-letter scrawl. It's time to write whole words and sentences, flowing together and spelt correctly.'

The sun breaks through and they both look up at the window, as if asking for a blessing from above. Now they will always remember the weather during this lesson: a sunny winter's morning.

The idea is for the boy to skip Grade One, but in practice Mr Java has set his sights much higher: straight to Grade Three! Grade Four! For years now, Mr Java has succeeded in keeping his boy away from all schools. Nursery school? Nonsense. 'Folding and plaiting won't get you through. Yes, plaiting liana to build rafts, but we don't need a Miss for that.' Mr Java is a specialist. As the girls never attended nursery school either and learnt the three Rs in the jungle, Mother wasn't too worried about Mr Java playing the schoolmaster at home. But now the authorities have started making enquiries. 'Isn't it time for a real school?' she asks every time she sees the two of them bent over the table together.

'Still too playful for a large class,' Mr Java wrote to the headmaster, 'with a disadvantageous birthday and allergic.' He doesn't trust the Dutch education system at all. 'The best school is the school of life.' What's more, he has time to give his boy more attention than any teacher. He'll hatch him out himself: this is his pupil! The result will astound them.

Mr Java picks a shining yellow pencil up from the table. A new pencil for a new lesson. 'This is a real Koh-I-Noor, the world's best pencil. No sea, no sweat, no tropical sun will wash away the graphite. What it writes stays written. You just have to learn to handle it. Inside its wooden case it seems so stiff, but in your hand it's as unpredictable as a snake. Now we're going to tame it.' He rolls the pencil down the palm of one hand and rubs it warm between them both. It gives off a smell of wood and fire. 'That's how you get a pencil in the right mood and it gives you a supple hand.' (The boy has known this trick since his first colouring box, but Mr Java believes in repetition. He demonstrates everything – not once, but a hundred times, until he can do it blind.) Then Mr Java flicks his hands to loosen his fingers and tugs them one at a time. After cracking every knuckle, he sticks his right middle finger in the air. 'This is a writer's bump,' he says, pointing to the bulge near the nail. 'A noble callus you will have to work hard to earn.' (Mr Java is fond of digression, he combines all of his teaching with practical lessons for life. The boy has to be able to survive in the world and, if you want to know who you're dealing with, it's advisable to look at people's fingers the first time you meet them. A splayed thumb? A building worker, you'll see. Coloured cuticles betray painters; red edges show butchers; black calluses, market gardeners; long fingers, physicians and pianists; jabbed and stabbed tips, seamstresses; but the white, pinched fingertip shows a tailor, who wears a thimble day in, day out ... 'When the police find a washed-up body, the first thing they do is look at the hands, then they already know the half of it.')

Mr Java lends out his middle finger for his pupil to feel. A true writer's finger. Nicotine yellow. The smoke curls up out of it. The finger is warm and muscular; years of accumulated experience shimmer under the callus. The writer's bump throbs, swells, glows ... turning into a volcano, a Krakatoa of knowledge. The boy is so shocked he scratches a cross on it with his thumbnail, like he does with his hives, to stop them itching. And that in turn shocks Mr Java, the hand lashes out ... the writer's callus burns on the boy's cheek.

'This will be your weapon,' Mr Java says, planting the pencil between the boy's clammy thumb and index finger and resting it on the middle finger, where the writer's bump must grow. An old hand leads a young hand over the page. A dot, a line, up and down from left to right. They write letters. The wooden sunbeam feels light. The letters thread together, crooked but solid, with flourishes and hooks and high strokes. This is cursive. The way Mr Java learnt it overseas, sloping letters with the wind at their back. And that is how his pupil will learn it . . . They write his name. The young hand resists . . .

Crack. The point breaks. See, he only has to look at things and they break.

'It's because you're no good with your hands, that's why you have to learn to write,' says Mr Java. 'You're predestined for brainwork.'

Suddenly the Koh-I-Noor feels like a lead weight.

—

They spend hours practising at the table. Knee to knee. Arm to arm, him with his Koh-I-Noor, Mr Java with his fountain pen. Writing, copying. The pupil imitates the teacher. Sloping more and more and with ever grander strokes. The pupil soaks it up. Short words. Long words. Words he only knows the sound of.

Mr Java says, 'Danger lurks in every word.' And he shows him where the danger is hiding. In letters that swallow each other up, or swap places under your hand. A small b that turns into a d. A big R that walks off in the wrong direction. An M that flips into a W. The letters have to take on a fixed form in his mind. He has to read them out loud. Imprint. Recognise. Chisel those letters. Trace them, the longest words, wherever he finds them, and then write the letters out again underneath in his own hand, joined up and sloping.

Just when the boy thinks he has got the knack of a difficult word, his pencil slips and the letters run off in the opposite direction. Mr Java is panting over his shoulder – the more mistakes he makes, the harder he breathes. His fists swell next to the exercise book, his knuckles get whiter and whiter . . . that too happens over and over. The boy wants to calm the fists beside him . . . to pat them. A kiss on the knuckle the blood is draining from, a kiss on that threatening sleeve.

'What are you doing?' Mr Java demands with a look of disgust. And he whacks his pupil back into line.

Pupil? He's not worth the name . . . When his ears are red enough, the pupil lets himself slide down under the table. A hedgehog would raise its spines, but he throws himself on his back like a dog.

'Get up or I'll kick you up!' Mr Java's shoes do what he says.

Groans under the table, but just as many above it: Mr Java plants his teeth in his own hand . . . he didn't mean it like that . . . 'Sorry, sorry, sorry.' He hits the tabletop. With remorse. Harder. Harder still . . . until the calluses on his fingers are boiling and he shuffles out of the room a broken man.

—

Wardrobe doors creak, coat hooks rattle and shoes fall on the floor. Mr Java is getting changed for the fresh air. After an outburst of rage, he has to go outdoors – doctor's orders. He's going to exercise the lifeboat horses. They, at least, obey his hand: horses, he can read and write . . .

—

An hour later Mr Java crunches into the sitting room, his trousers covered with splashed-up sand. Before he's had time to get changed, his pupil throws himself into his arms. Two hands dig into the boy's curls, pushing his face into the elbow of the horse-riding coat. Mr Java makes him sniff it up until, coughing, he fights his way free. Educator is his true profession. He does it with hand and soul.

the difference

Mr Java has been to the city, a day in the crowds: arranging things, documents and pension stuff, long queues at lots of counters. 'I made an important discovery today,' he says at the dinner table.

What?

Mr Java keeps quiet.

The family is all ears. Spoons stick in dishes, plates stay half filled. 'First you tickle our curiosity and then you clam up. Come on, tell us.'

Mr Java pretends he hasn't heard. He's been acting strange since he got home. Preoccupied, not interested in anything around him. Mother can make a mash out of dinner, the girls can be messy and he hardly notices the boy. No radio. He hasn't even touched the paper. You can't make him angry. When dinner is finally dished up, the boy scrapes his knife over his plate — to draw some words out of him — and Mr Java says quietly, 'My eyes are too slow, everyone else sees things faster.'

41

'What are you talking about?' asks Mother.

'I noticed on the train,' Mr Java continues hesitantly, 'flashing eyes, everywhere I looked, and later in town, the speed with which people there see things: register, evaluate, walk on. Ferret eyes. It took me a long time to catch on, but now I know for sure: I'm suffering from slow eyes. They don't look, they suck tight. And they don't let go. The stuff I lug around with me! Entire portrait galleries, an atlas of landscapes. I'd like to erase most of the pictures, but everything I've seen just hangs there ... Weighing me down. Quick eyes see lighter, I see it in you too: *click click* go those lashes. Snaps you can just forget again. I should have realised sooner ... That's why we understand each other worse and worse. Your pupils dance, mine get stiffer and stiffer.'

The family tries to look him in the eye. What nonsense. The girls put on finger glasses. Mother fetches a hand mirror. Noses press against noses.

'It's the crux of my problem,' Mr Java sighs with his eyes raised to heaven.

The family follows his gaze on its journey around the room (glancing back to calculate the slowness of his pupils) until all eyes have come to rest above the motionless flowers in the motionless damask.

'Haven't you noticed it before?' he asks Mother.

'You're imagining things.'

'Because you look faster, you're only aware of half of what you experience.'

'If only,' she mocks.

'And you?' Mr Java asks the girls. 'Didn't you notice anything back then?'

The girls giggle. No, they haven't forgotten the first time they saw him. And it's true, they didn't look properly at all. It took them months to discover his terrible bandy legs – on a cold Dutch beach – but back then, just after the war, they were blinded by the sharp creases in his trousers. They saw him every day at the Red Cross: he was searching a list for his wife; they were searching for their father, a name without a face. They had been waiting for a sign of life since the end of the war, it had been months and months. And suddenly that man appeared in the queue, a man who was overflowing with plans and jokes . . . At the time every girl was longing for a father. That's hard to imagine now . . .

Mother and the girls slide closer together. So much is coming back to them . . . The boy slips off his chair and tries to wedge in between them. They don't make room, they don't even notice him, and merge as a single back. 'That was before your time,' they say, 'you weren't even born then.'

Mr Java gazes blankly past their black hair – black with a blue sheen. At the table eyes flee from eyes, but memories shoot back and forth: no, not in the old days, in the old days they didn't notice anything weird about him at all.

'And you?' Mr Java asks Mother. 'Why are you so quiet . . .'

She shakes herself free from the girls' cuddles and shrugs irritably. 'If your eyes are so slow: there's a letter here from the schools inspector that came weeks ago.'

Dear Sirs

Dear Sirs,

We would like to take this opportunity to inform you that our family is at death's door . . .

Mr Java writes a letter. Out loud. *Dear Sirs, Although I do not like to make a habit of repeatedly . . .* There are so many Dear Sirs that Mother complains about the stamps. The Dear Sirs of Banka-Billiton, the Dear Sirs of Java Tobacco, the Dear Sirs of the Deli Railway Company. Famous names, exclusive addresses . . . but that's as far as it goes. They're all shysters, leeches, defaulters! And Mr Java makes sure they know it. Once these gentlemen promised him the moon – and not just him. He has brought out the stock box again, to count the coupons properly once and for all, noting the code numbers and the dates of payment. 'Lapsed, according to these gentlemen, expired, but not on my calendar!'

The boy only half listens to Mr Java's tirades; he picks out the most beautiful pictures for tracing: palm trees, a smoking volcano, steamships, locomotives, squatting women with tobacco-leaf hats — it's not often the stock box appears on the table.

Mr Java nudges the boy: 'It says it here, in black and white, in words and numbers ... plain as the nose on your face.' Proof flutters over the table — shares, vouchers, bearer bonds ... creased, stained, tearing at the folds. Smoked fingers tap the signatures, the stamps and the brown carbons from the Restitution Board.

Restitution ... a word that trembles through the whole room. Fresh from the box, it hides anxiously under the lampshade ... but later in the afternoon, when Mr Java has taken over the entire tablecloth and pulled out even more documents, when he is laying out his cigarettes and writing paper, filling his pens with poison ink, pulling the starched cuffs of his shirt down over his wrists, yes, then he impales the word on his nib. Sometimes it puts up a struggle and he fights with it — it can curse, weep and smudge — at other times it sings and laughs. Restitution. The boy has traced it and, by the end of a long afternoon, he can write it perfectly, sloping, from beginning to end and back again, upside-down if necessary. It's a wonderful word, *restitution*. And a delight to say: it cools the tongue, it purses the lips. After restitution everything will be perfect again. After restitution roast chickens will fly over the table. After restitution a light-blue Buick will drive down the boulevard. And who will be in it? Mr Java and his boy! After restitution Mother and the girls will wear furs, there will

46

be a fire in every room and . . . finally, finally, after hundreds of letters to council and county, it will be possible to flush the toilet with paper and all (poo paper now goes into a separate bucket). The house will smell lovely after restitution.

But first the letters and the proof. *Dear Sirs, enclosed, please find* . . . Mr Java has had copies made. They've come out splodgy and as thick as a lampshade. Of course, he would never surrender the originals. And definitely not the most fragile documents, the ones the boy is not even allowed to look at: the papers from the Pepper Gardens have been in the family for years. He keeps the pepper papers in separate folders and scrubs his hands before briefly exposing them to light. Not too long, that would bleach the gallnut ink even more. These proofs are pale brown, decked out with orange stamps with embossed white crowns . . . and flourishing at the bottom are the signatures of the gentlemen, half mouldered away, eroded by rust, termites and floods, but still legible. And that's what matters! Mr Java carried their names against his chest through the jungle, he buried them deep under the ground in an iron box. And what do the battered papers show? 'Misappropriation! These gentlemen's management! All gone on administration costs during my' – for a moment Mr Java has to gasp for breath – 'absence.' And afterwards as well: proceeds nil. And not because Batavia was suddenly called Jakarta and the guilder suddenly became the rupiah! Did the pepper stop flowering all those years? Did the coolies refuse to pick it? And what about the nutmeg, the tobacco, the tea? Did they stop shelling coffee beans as well, did the rubber trees run dry, and what about the packet boats, the railways, the Batavian Petroleum Company, the Javanese . . . ? Mr Java bangs down the lid. 'Peace didn't come cheap.' But next year . . . after restitution. Next week, maybe tomorrow . . .

Mr Java's writing hand races over the paper. This time he'll show those gentlemen. Line after line flows out of his pen. He doesn't hesitate or repeat himself. He doesn't smudge, his margin is as straight as an arrow (that's how the writer shows his character: straightforward, true). A mysterious smile appears on his lips. His eyes flash. 'Ooh, that will hit home, see how they like that one . . .' Or, 'No, that's too insulting . . .' Screw it up into a ball and take another clean sheet. Mr Java uses each cigarette to light the next, he talks smoke. He rubs the gentlemen's noses in the facts: didn't the minister state shortly after the war . . . wasn't a promise made on Free Dutch Radio that . . . and wasn't a financial arrangement going to be made to . . . The most difficult words fly over the net tablecloth. Mother hushes and quenches him with cups of tea and drops of bromide, terrified that the pepper papers will get Mr Java overheated.

After an ashtray full of butts and a waste-paper basket full of balls of paper, Mr Java's *Dear Sir* curses diminish to a whisper. Does the big-shot director remember how he went on board? Skinny and dirty like all the rest, he had to stand in line for a berth. Almost in his birthday suit, but he wasn't born yesterday ... And the airs he gave himself! Before you knew it, he was at the front of the queue. They knew each other from their younger years, from the racetrack: he had been an excellent horseman, cunning even then. Mr Java had lent him his linen suit right there on the dock – white with a high, stiff collar – picked up from a Chinese after intense haggling. No Europeans had anything like it so soon after the war! The big-shot director bent over backwards trying to convince him: if he could just borrow that suit for a while, just for the voyage, a man in his position ... to dine with the captain, for business over billiards ... he'd pay him for it when they arrived.

Mr Java growls at the memory. His pen hangs idly in his hand.

And what did the gentleman get on board? His own cabin. Upper deck. He never came below. Never said hello, never said anything. Disembarked with a lady he'd met on board. In *his* suit!

'Many claims are yet to be settled,' says Mr Java.

He slides back his chair and walks to the window. A strange movement creeps into his legs, as if he's at sea again, he presses his forehead against the glass and mists his view with his own breath ... he wipes the window clean. As silently as his breath settled on the glass, that's how loudly it squeaks when he wipes it away. 'Full moon,' he whispers.

He turns on his heel and leaves the room.

The boy is upset by his abrupt departure. It is quiet, very quiet. As if the whole house is on tiptoe. He pricks up his ears ... and hears the creaking of a wardrobe door, feet sliding over tiles, a coat hanger clattering on the floor. He imagines what Mr Java is doing in the other rooms: pressing a pair of trousers – *hissss, hissss* – with a razor-sharp crease, brushing off his best suit, picking out a thick scarf, pinning on his medals in preparation. Mr Java takes his leather briefcase, the case he often takes when he goes to put things right. The letter case. Mr Java gets ready for a journey to the Dear Sirs. Maybe tomorrow he'll visit the minister ...

But ... he doesn't unfold the ironing board, the tea towel doesn't hiss under the iron. Rubber galoshes squeak in the hall and suddenly Mr Java is standing in the sitting room, hat on his head, two oilskins over one arm. Mother scurries up behind. 'Come on, a little sea air will do us good,' he says. Mother gestures furiously behind his back ... Out, out, take him out with you, her hands say. Mr Java hangs the smallest coat over the narrowest shoulders and zips it up in a single tug.

'My arms,' the boy squeaks.

'Don't need 'em.' Mr Java slips his coat on and inspects his pockets.

Mother quickly puts a pair of rubber boots ready and digs up the thickest scarf she can find. The smell of mothballs itches through the room. The boy sneezes.

'Blow your nose,' Mr Java says distractedly. He finds a compass in his pocket and holds it up to one ear. It's still got north in it.

The boy flaps his empty sleeves, shuffles along with his heels half-way up his boots and wipes his nose on the scarf.

—

They take the quickest route to the beach, straight through the dunes. The bunkers cast round shadows over their path, giant helmets in the moonlight. Mr Java gives his boy a hand and together they eat their way through the darkness.

The beach is lighter, a yellow strip beside a sleeping sea – the moon has room to shine. No waves, no lapping; a modest east wind has silenced the surf. They walk along the frothy edge of the sea, towards the moon, heading south – the pre-war south. The world seems empty and peaceful. A crab scuttles off. They listen to their splashing steps. Alongside each other, the same leg forward, feet synchronised. Two shadows follow behind. 'Two big shots,' whispers Mr Java. He kicks them away. One shadow kicks too. Mr Java waves, one shadow waves with him. Mr Java takes off his hat, two hats salute the moon. The boy's shadow stays mute beside him. 'Polite gentlemen,' says Mr Java, 'but keep your eye on them, they'll cheat you as soon as look at you.' Then he pulls the boy up against him . . . and together they look back at the shadow, standing behind them now like one man. 'See, you can't even trust your own shadow. One minute it's walking along behind you, the next it's left you in the lurch.' Mr Java puts his hand on the boy's neck and together they bow to their shadow. 'Before you know it, you get swallowed up and then you're less than nothing.' A sudden wind comes up, the sea drowns out the whispering . . . but the words hit home.

Suddenly Mr Java leaps away: he and his shadow splash through the wet sand. Mr Java transforms himself into a knife. He slashes at his shadow. Arms and legs fall on to the sand. A cloud slides in front of the moon. Mr Java no longer has a shadow. He's trampling his own body under his feet. Mr Java is no longer himself.

lesson for life

Next to the paddock there is a bare birch, a tough and springy thing, branches too thin for climbing, but a natural catapult. Before the top's down on the ground the birch will have to bend low. Who dares?

The boy jumps into the tree, pulls himself up, clamps the trunk between his legs and scrapes his way up gnarl by gnarl. The higher he gets, the thinner the trunk. The birch trembles, tries to shake him off, leans over . . . and . . . surrenders. His feet touch the ground again. Hold that trunk, push it down, grab it by the crown, don't let it go. And now a shoe, who's got a shoe? A ring of eyes weighs up each boy's shoes: the others are urchins from the other side of the village . . . His! Yes, his. The birch conqueror himself must surrender a shoe. The boys point at him, at his Norwegian hikers, no one has anything as beautiful – sturdy, bought to grow into. Not exactly bought, they were donated, but nobody's allowed to know that. They look brand spanking new. And expensive! Expensive! They tie his right shoe loosely to the top of the tree with the lace. And now, back up, boys . . .

press the trunk down a little bit longer . . . And one, two . . . three! *Thwoop* . . . The tree goes berserk. What a launch. The shoe shoots through the air. The shoe floats . . . High. Like a rocket. What a laugh. Where's it gone? Searching. Nowhere in sight. Not in the grass, not in the ditch.

And then?

Hop home in one shoe – as if he's in pain. Point at the guilty ones – as if he's been robbed.

—

'What's going to become of you?' asks Mr Java, who was waiting for him at the window. 'How long do you think you'll last with just one shoe?' His eyes are impassive, his voice sounds cold. 'What kind of state will you be in after marching five hundred miles? With a wrecked foot on the frozen mud? Your flesh ripped off, to the bone . . . They won't wait for you, the group keeps moving. You can't go on and your so-called comrades become dots on a grey plain. It gets even colder, biting snowstorms . . . You hear that? Wolves, wolves out on the steppe. No – it's howling jet fighters . . . There, behind the trees.' Mr Java points at the ceiling and the boy looks up and sees them – black fighters! 'Tackatackatackatack . . . a trail of bullets racing down the road, hit the ground. Take cover. Run through the snow, jump over barbed wire, dive behind a tree. Ha-ha . . . Your leg won't run. Numb. Gangrene. Yeah, just sit down . . . Want to be carried,

I suppose, by me, in my condition! The burden that you are. No-hoper. Why did you get two shoes, two first-class hiking boots? Because you've got two feet, two feet on two legs, your own two feet. Two feet to stand on. Feet that don't need anyone else. Feet that need to be ready to go. Weakling.'

Two eyes cower before him. The boy is silent.

'If you let your shoes get stolen you were a dead man,' Mr Java adds after an icy silence.

Fear oozes through a single sock.

'Unless you had footpower.' Mr Java looks at the boy's trail of sweat and sniggers at his own words. 'Footpower!' His laughter melts the snow in his voice. He slaps his knees with delight.

The boy doesn't understand why.

the newspaper

Every evening the lies fall on the mat. And every time the boy finds strange words to write in his exercise book. Until Mr Java takes the newspaper from the boy, smooths it out, fluffs it up and reads from it, hissing, sneering and ranting, 'Lies, all lies.' But everyone still has to listen every evening: to how much drivel distant officials are talking and how senile old men are drawing new borders and changing the map so often he might just as well buy a new atlas every month, look how they've squandered Asia, and keep an eye on the Chinese, they're suspiciously quiet . . . and power-mad Russians will steal the horses from the barns . . .

'Shut up!' screams Mother.

And then it's quiet.

Chairs slide over the floor and Mr Java and Mother assume their positions. Mother takes her knitting and Mr Java hides behind an open newspaper – the pages shake in his hands – and everyone in the house knows what they're not talking about: the bomb.

The Americans' new super-destructive hydrogen bomb.

But not for long.

Mr Java is for and Mother's against.

'You owe it your life,' Mr Java repeats. He can't say it often enough.

'Hiroshima and Nagasaki brought peace. Two atom bombs were enough. The H-bomb is much bigger.'

'Let the Russians tremble,' Mr Java insists. After a hot war, he can take a cold one in his stride.

'It only takes *one* mad general,' Mother says. 'They already play with it like a toy, in Australia they've obliterated entire islands and God knows what they get up to in Siberia . . . Inventions get used and we'll end up paying the price.' Since the communists have had an atomic bomb of their own, she has almost become a pacifist. 'An even more terrible mushroom cloud will leave the earth scorched.'

Mr Java: 'What do you want us to do? Let them lock us up?'

'The fallout can get you anywhere.' Mother knows just what a hydrogen bomb can do, she saw a photo in a magazine: an H-bomb on Dam Square in Amsterdam would wipe out all of North Holland . . . 'including our village, this house, incinerated, flat . . . in a flash of light.'

'If it comes to that, I will personally dig out the cellar.'

'And you: vaporised.'

'We'll see who's the strongest.'

'The cockroaches.'

'Nonsense,' says Mr Java. He knows much more about it than she does. Every day he goes to the hotel on the boulevard and reads as many newspapers as he likes, national and international, *Life* and *Time*, all for the price of a pot of coffee. He knows exactly what they're getting up to behind the Iron Curtain and what the Americans think of it. 'Life will be quite possible after the bomb.'

'As long as you've got enough peanut butter stocked up,' Mother mocks.

'That's right, with lots of jars of peanut butter and tins of beans and sugar and plum pudding and kerosene . . . and if you don't stop whining about it, I'll go out tomorrow and buy another gross.' Mr Java dares to say all this as long as he's hiding behind the newspaper.

Mother throws a skein of wool at his head.

'Maybe we should build up a new existence some-where else. A better existence, safer. A hydrogen bomb will actually scorch the earth clean . . . as clean as a whistle.' He lets the wool roll down his legs and goes looking for the scissors.

Mr Java clips the paper. The lies go into the lie envelope. For the boy, he cuts out pictures of jet fighters. He's in luck today . . . there's a pilot too, in a rugged jacket, standing proud next to his little P–38, the plane the Yanks used to shoot the Japanese out of the sky. By scratching the back of the photo with his Koh-I-Noor, the boy prints the pilot's reflection in his exercise book. Grey on white, softer than in the paper. He has often made mirror images of words and pictures from newspapers and magazines, but this print is especially clear: the pilot's collar is as fluffy as real life and his lips look just like lips. The mirror pilot smiles at him . . . if he stares at him long enough he even moves . . . For a second it looked like he was raising his thumb.

—

Every evening Mr Java and Mother bicker about the bomb. The A-bomb and the H-bomb. The world is split in two, and so is the sitting room. The boy doesn't know who to seek shelter with.

changes

New trousers, new pullover, new shoes, new jacket. Mr Java has capitulated: next week the boy goes to school after all. One term late. The clothes are laid out on the cabin trunk. New clothes for a pupil who can already read and write. The boy keeps going in to check them. He likes the jacket the most: thick brown cotton with black woollen cuffs and a fluffy, upright collar. He spent days begging for it and finally Mother made it. When he puts it on, he looks just like the American mirror pilot in his exercise book.

The school is four miles away, almost as far as the girls' secondary school – like them, he won't be able to come home for lunch. He is already saying goodbye to the secrets in the house, inspecting familiar routes, as if the places he touches in passing – sometimes closing his eyes to make a wish – are about to lose their power. The bike scratches in the plaster in the hall, the loose skirting board, the bookcase where he can always find something that needs straightening . . . Mother won't recognise his secret codes and signals, she'll tidy up his room. She will take a wet cloth and wipe away the letters he scratched in the geranium pots with his fingernail.

Mr Java is gloomy as well. The primary education inspector had written to inform him (to warn him, according to Mother) that the boy had to go to school immediately and that no classes could be skipped without the permission of the head teacher. 'What a country,' Mr Java rages. 'What busybodies! After all our hard work!'

'We're not ready yet,' he wrote back, but the inspector was implacable. This or that law stipulated that everyone had to stick to the same rules.

'They're breeding sheep.' Don't they know what that leads to?

—

Mr Java misses his son already, sitting right next to him: while writing, he wraps an arm around his pupil – for no reason – and smooths down his curls, almost choking him and leaving him gasping for breath. 'Sorry,' he says, slapping the boy on the back of the head where his hair has already been shaved up high in preparation for the first day of school. The boy is going to miss him too. Who will sharpen his pencils for him at school?

After the lesson, Mr Java stands in front of the window like an *A* (feet apart, arms crossed) and mumbles inaudibly to himself . . . until dots of froth start appearing in the corners of his mouth and Mother sends him out of the room.

Before dinner, when he has calmed down again, he says solemnly, 'I thought about it some more. If I change the horse schedule, we can still read and write together for an hour after school.'

This as a counterbalance: support and comfort.

—

The day before school the boy is all nerves, in and out of his bedroom to inspect his school clothes. Mother has laid a pair of matching socks with the rest and Mr Java has added an unsharpened Koh-I-Noor. All new. In these clothes, he can become someone else. Equipped like this, he dares to go into battle. Gently stroking the jacket, he automatically straightens his back and sees himself fearlessly crossing the playground.

'Why don't you put it on now?' asks Mother.

'It's raining,' he says, but thinks, Not yet, otherwise the power will go out of it.

She looks out of the window. 'It's only spitting, I made it for weather like this.'

'I'd rather just wear my old coat.'

'You're an ungrateful child.'

—

The mirror pilot says, 'She doesn't feel the newness, the completeness. For her a jacket is a jacket, a shell to keep out the wind and rain. She doesn't understand that clothes can turn you into a new boy.'

the dud

There's a bomb under the boulevard. In the middle of the village, opposite the marine aquarium. Workers digging up the road with picks heard a clang, iron on iron. It went right through them. They thought it was a tank trap, a remnant of the Atlantic Wall, or a shot-down Allied bomber, but it turned out to be a bomb, a British bomb from World War II, they've laid it completely bare, six foot long – from nose to tail – and apart from a few scratches perfectly intact. Six foot. The whole village is talking about it. Six foot! Men, women and children tell each other how big with amazement. Six foot. Mr Java paces it out on the brown lino, six times his shoe plus one big step. A bomb as big as a tall man. And dangerous! That thing's not dead, it's dormant, inside it's ready to go. Digging it up to defuse it somewhere else is too risky. There's a risk of spontaneous detonation. Det-o-na-tion . . . First-class word! Mr Java spells it out, writes it in the exercise book, his eyes flash. That word's got sound in it: a high, whistling tone. Mr Java whistles. It sounds like a wood pigeon, a big fat one. Why didn't the bomb explode? 'It was a dud, swallowed up by the sand.'

Mr Java knows what he's talking about: since the boy started school, he's spent every morning at the hotel reading table. No news of war can escape him there, neither domestic nor international, he even dirties his hands on German newspapers. He knows all the hot spots. What's more, he was already a bomb specialist. People ask him about it, on the street, on the beach, he draws aircraft with the end of his cane – he's brought it out with him for the occasion, the cane is his outdoor pen. 'Look,' he says, 'this is the altitude and this is the belly of the plane, the target is here, at this angle . . .' People out walking dogs, policemen, the grocer, cyclists from other villages . . . they form a circle around him, following the tip of his cane, in the sand, on stone or up in the air. Yes, they can hear it . . . the unexploded bomb is on everyone's mind.

And what happens now? Distance and control are Mr Java's unsolicited recommendations. First measure: the boy can stay home from school, the cycle path is too close to the bomb. The girls ignore his advice and go their own way. But the mayor takes Mr Java's side and sends a car through the streets with a crackling megaphone to warn the residents: 'Avoid the boulevard. Stay away from windows!' A British army captain has been flown over as well – a bomb specialist with hundreds of successful explosions to his name. He will detonate the bomb on the spot. Farmer Joe has stacked two hundred bales of straw around the hole, just in case . . . because if it blows, the aquarium will go. The shark will come wriggling out. Sea-horses galloping along behind. Imagine. Creamed anemone on the window ledge. It doesn't bear thinking about, says Mr Java.

The boy can't think about anything else. If he hears Mr Java whistle — there's always a newcomer who hasn't heard the story — and looks up in the sky, he sees starfish whizzing by . . . buzzing electric eels, stingrays, gasping swordfish . . . an airborne aquarium on the blast from the bomb. After the straw, they dumped four tons of sand in front of the entrance to the building, all to temper the force of the explo-sion. They've even opened the Peace Chapel — the pastor provides counselling. Yes, the war is ticking away under the sand.

Mother went into the chapel. The whole village was squeezed in there. But Mr Java made a point of waiting outside. He is definitely not scared. Self-control! But he still has a bag ready at home with clean under-wear, bromide drops, the photo album and his gold cufflinks (for bribes). And he has rummaged through his secret boxes: a pile of documents must come too. 'The pepper papers, yes?' He tosses the letters from the tax department carelessly in a corner; worries can be left behind. 'Ignoring is bliss,' he chortles. They pack together, as father and son — that's how it feels, in these exciting hours the boy is a part of it all, he gets to put his things in the bag as well: blank exercise books, three brand-new Koh-I-Noors. The bag goes under the bed while they wait for new instructions. How often Mr Java has mapped out their path to safer shores, where tanks can't follow, out of range of bombs and rockets. Distance!

The *kepten* – as the village calls the British bomb captain – is staying at the hotel; not in a room, a whole floor has been cordoned off just for him, as if he might explode as well. People wait outside in front of the door, complete strangers with cameras on straps on their stomachs, pointing up at windows where they think they've caught a glimpse of their hero. The *kepten* paces back and forth. The *kepten* bends over old blueprints. The *kepten* comes up with a plan. The *kepten* sits down at the table. The *kepten* eats. No, he doesn't eat: a *kepten* breakfasts, lunches and dines. The mayor has been to visit him with a bottle of the best red wine.

Since the *kepten*'s arrival, Mr Java has been practising his English. *How do you do, captain?* He studies his English tweed, his English hat, his English tie and his English shoes in the mirror. *Yes, I would like to speak the captain*. Mr Java has seen plenty of bombs fall. Four-footers, five-footers . . . right in front of his nose. Not little ones, *big boys*. The stud was blown up, his ship was torpedoed . . . and now he's singing about the bomb. He hasn't been in such a good mood for months. *Bom-B. Bom-B*. A *B* at the front, a *B* behind, it makes a bang coming and going. What a word! *Bombbombbom-B* . . . Mr Java teaches his son English: *Tally-ho, big bomb-B show* . . . The bomb booms from their lips.

'He's got better things to do,' says Mother.

'I want to thank him.'

'Interrupt him, more like.'

Mr Java has bought a bottle of his own for the *kepten*, more expensive than the mayor's wine, ruby port. An officer drinks port, with his left hand, to honour Admiral Nelson who lost his right arm at Trafalgar. Blown off by a cannon-ball. Mother thinks it's a dangerous gift. 'That man has to keep a cool head, he needs two right hands.' Mr Java wipes the dust off the label. 'At most, this port will touch his heart.' 'And the bottom of my housekeeping purse,' is Mother's dry response. They argue about who really liberated them: the Allies, but does that include the Russians? War talk ricochets round the room, strange, new words are spelt out and written down. These are highly educational days!

He has to hand over the port before the det-o-na-tion. As soon as possible! Because the rumour is going around that it could happen any moment . . . The boy can come too. (If there is one occasion on which he should wear his flying jacket, this is it: the *kepten* was a pilot too. Rugged, with the collar turned up . . . the jacket goes on and off four times, collar up, collar down – he's too scared, he strokes the material, it calms him down again and he finds the courage, but every time he steps out into the hall he is overcome by a strange fear. 'Go on,' the mirror pilot whispers finally in his ear – his voice is in the collar – and there he goes, with pounding heart.)

Mr Java is waiting impatiently, but he is too preoccupied by the bottle of port to pay attention to his son . . . In a bag or not, gift-wrapped or unwrapped, in his left hand or in his right? Finally he cradles it in his left arm, rolled up in a thick newspaper – it is a precious child, this bottle – the boy can carry the cane. A cane that rattles fearlessly over fences on the way and stabs into bales of straw, until Mr Java grabs it and raps him with it. 'And turn down that collar.' Self-control, that's what matters now they're approaching the *kepten*! So: no sneezing, no scratching, back straight and don't drag your feet.

An inquisitive throng is gathered outside the hotel – they too have heard the rumour. Mr Java, the cane, the bottle and the boy push their way to the front without incident, but two policemen block the entrance. Do they have an appointment? *Yes.* Do they know the *kepten* personally? *Yes.* The policemen almost bow.

Mr Java whistles under his breath as he steps through the revolving door. This is *his* hotel, where he reads the morning and foreign papers every day and is served coffee in a silver pot – with three biscuits included in the price. The wind catches his coat and his chin goes up a little, his whole face takes on an air the boy has never seen before . . . his step on the bare marble sounds confident, he doesn't skid along like the boy, who has never been inside before: hotels are for holidaymakers and this one is reserved for the wealthiest. Mr Java greets the staff – a man in a pink-striped waistcoat who is emptying an ashtray and a lady in a white apron who flaps her red nails at him strangely in reply. He holds his coat, hat and cane out to a lady with an enormous bosom, who seizes them as if she undresses Mr Java every day . . . no, the boy's not silly, he's keeping his jacket on. Mr Java chats to the bosom and when the boy tugs on his sleeve, he quickly points out the five brass clocks over the desk, each of which shows a different time. That's what it's like in the big wide world, each continent has its own time. And Mr Java knows that world.

But the face under the clocks does not react to his jovial greeting. A man in a coat with gold embroidered keys on the collar frowns at them. Mr Java hands him his visiting card with one corner folded over, the boy spells a word that is carved into the desk: con . . . cier . . . ge . . . 'The *kepten* is unable to receive visitors,' says the concierge. Mr Java clicks his English shoes together, clears his throat and pulls the port out of the newspaper . . . it fails to impress.

'The *kepten* is a tea drinker,' says the concierge. A

little patience and the *kepten* will come out and then everyone can see him. 'It's scheduled for four o'clock.' His hands imitate an explosion.

Mr Java points out the label, the port is from the year of liberation. The concierge is implacable, his head disappears in the guest book. Mr Java puts the bottle down on the marble desk and slides it into the lamp-light, under the nose of the concierge. Not a peep. When he abandons the bottle and goes to pick up his coat, his English clothes are hanging loose on his body . . . *Tweed-tweed* rasps the fabric under his arms as he steps into the revolving door. Mr Java is not whistling now, he is deflating.

But outside, in front of the waiting crowd, he pumps himself up again. 'The *kepten* is getting ready, it will be a little later: four o'clock, local time.' Mr Java taps on the glass of his wristwatch and waves his cane. 'First-hand information,' he says, nodding at the policemen. The concierge grins through the window. 'Four o'clock, four o'clock . . .' a whisper passes through the rows, 'local time.' 'Where's that?' asks a high voice from between the hats and raincoats.

A little later the car with the megaphone confirms it loudly in the streets. '*Avoid danger, stay away from the boulevard.*' A vigil will be held in the Peace Chapel. With the pastor's wife serving hot chocolate. And those who insist on seeing something have to climb the high dune: only there, safe behind a buffer of sand, can you . . . yes, what? . . . see a puff of sand and a shadowy shoulder, maybe. 'Not for us,' says Mr Java. 'Nothing but morbid curiosity.'

On the way home his son turns around at least five times. The high dune beckons, the high dune entices . . . Mr Java brushes a straw from his tweed. 'If it goes wrong, we'll hear it on the radio.' Anyway, he doesn't want to get his clothes all sandy.

At home Mother is making her own plans. The girls are back from school early and want to go to the vigil. 'Everyone will be there,' says Mother, 'it will be nice.'

'Not us,' says Mr Java, 'only dead fish go with the flow.'

Mother and the girls withdraw into the bedroom.

'Pyjamas,' he orders his son.

What? This early? That's ridiculous! It's the middle of the afternoon! And what if the detonation goes wrong and they have to leave the house? Fleeing in pyjamas?

Mr Java refuses to take no for an answer. He's going to make sandwiches, nobody is going to feel like cooking today. He slices a whole loaf, then interrupts his sandwich-spreading to walk from the kitchen into the sitting room, look out and slide the radio further away from the window.

Mother and the girls giggle behind a closed door and reappear, dressed not for bed, but for church: woollen stockings, cardigans, thick socks. They brush their teeth in the bathroom. Put on lipstick and sing harmonies: '*There floats through the clouds the loveliest name . . .*' Mr Java bites his lower lip.

The giggling moves outside. Heels join other heels, muffled voices walk past, bicycle bells catch up with bicycle bells, a moped, a car beeps in the distance . . . they're all going.

Mr Java tries to find a radio station, paces through the house, stands in front of the window, fiddles with the penknife in his pocket. The boy sits at the table in his pyjamas with wet hair and leafs through his exercise book. The mirror pilot offers no advice.

Mr Java takes off his shoes, pulls on slippers, does a circuit of the house, reaches into the chest of drawers . . . another pair of shoes, climbing shoes! Trousers off. He shakes out the creases and hangs them up – sand falls on the lino. Another pair of trousers go on, a pair without turn-ups. Climbing shoes on. The clock ticks.

The binoculars come out of their case. Mr Java wipes the lenses and inspects the sky, he turns and searches . . . scanning the windows. The binoculars imprint two rings around his eyes, like the dents in the velvet case. The boy follows the restless binoculars. Out of sight of those extended eyes, he creeps to his room, pulls trousers and a pullover on over his pyjamas . . . socks, shoes. And the flying jacket, collar up – in one go. When he returns to the sitting room fully dressed, Mr Java is tying himself in knots in front of the window, trying to look around a corner.

But the binoculars refuse to play along, they want to see as much as possible, outside the house, and the further the better. The binoculars pull Mr Java out by the strap and drag the boy along as well. They want to go to the boulevard, but by the back way, straight through the marram grass and up the climbing dune, forcing their way in between elbows, broad backs and farmers' caps . . . until they're standing firm with a clear view of the ring of bales. Two lenses become one and descend into the excavated hole . . . where they find the bomb . . . quiet and motionless, like a patient on an operating table.

The bomb is a rusty sausage in a sandpit. Nothing is happening. The binoculars seek the *kepten*, sweeping over to the hotel and back again. They seek the Peace Chapel – a vague stained light between the pines. The sun has already disappeared behind the high dune, a wintry grey colours the sky.

Mr Java has trouble keeping up with the binoculars, his greedy eyes race over the darkening village . . . roofs spin, streets squirm . . . it makes him dizzy and he leans on the boy . . . until the binoculars pull him back up on to his feet. A man is walking there, two legs in uniform. Got him! Don't let him slip away. The *kepten*'s steady pace – straight to the bales of straw. He's carrying a case, the det-o-na-tion case . . . a policeman is walking behind him. Is he seeing right? The policeman is carrying something else. Something small. What is it, what is it? The people nudge each other. Mr Java has to tell them what he sees.

He sees a bottle. He sees a bucket.

The *kepten* sits down on a bale and rolls up his sleeves. Mr Java squints, adjusts the focus of the binoculars, turns the wheel and swears. He stands on his toes and strains his eyes. Yes, the other people on the dune can see it now as well. The policeman has a bottle of wine in his hand . . . he pours the wine into the bucket . . . or is it port?

'What a waste!'

'The *kepten*'s washing his hands in the bucket.'

'He's taking a long time about it.'

'The *kepten*'s thinking.'

'He's not washing his hands, he's soaking them!'

'In wine?'

'He's making his fingers supple.'

The onlookers are left guessing. Mr Java's eyes burn through the lenses. Is it wine? Is it port?

More police arrive. They drag the bales of straw some distance from the bomb, build a hut and make themselves scarce. The *kepten* stands up, climbs down to the bomb with his case. He bends, he fiddles with something . . .

The dune holds its breath.

The *kepten* flaps his hands. Hands of salvation.

After this great gesture, he jumps out of the hole and withdraws to the hut of straw.

The *kepten* counts his seconds.

Mr Java counts out loud. The whole dune counts along.

From far away comes singing . . . psalms from the Peace Chapel . . . but loudest of all is the silence: creaking in the wheel between the binoculars' lenses, smacking in dry mouths, gurgling in excited tummies, sliding past trousers, boots and high collars, under warm armpits. The silence crunches in every ear . . . so nervously and for so long that no one hears the bang.

It wasn't even a bang, it was a vibration.

A fountain of sand.

Sand sprays over the boulevard, over the bales of straw, against the shop windows. Sand that blocks sight and smothers sound. No one's seen a thing. Not even the binoculars. The dune is enveloped in a cloud of sand.

Mr Java blows the lenses clean. The air clears. Sound returns. The *kepten* crawls out from under the straw. He brushes off the sand.

The church doors swing open, women and children run to the boulevard, men and boys run down the dune. Everyone wants to see the crater up close. Cameras are pulled out. The *kepten* puts his arm around anyone who wants a photo. The flash reflects on his teeth. He says cheese. The village breathes a sigh of relief. '*Tally-ho, good show,*' whispers the mirror pilot in the boy's collar.

Mr Java rakes through the straw around the crater with his cane, looking for shrapnel. The pieces are too hot to pick up, he flicks them with the end of his cane and they fall steaming in the cold sand. Torches search them out, boys pick up the pieces with handkerchiefs, blowing on them. Suddenly everyone wants to take a bit of bomb home with them. Men, women and children crawl over the sand. Mr Java hesitates, growls, bends . . . he slips a piece of shrapnel into his tweed pocket.

—

The next day the souvenir hunters wake up with bloody hands. It seems the pieces contain a slow-working acid. The car with the megaphone drives through the streets again. Don't panic: a dermatologist will come to check their wounds.

'Their fingers will be itching from the war for a long time yet,' the *kepten* tells a reporter from the evening paper.

Mr Java is scratching all week.

materialisation

Mr Java is standing in the middle of the path in front of the house. Quarter past four in the afternoon, school's finished, the boy and the girls ride up bunched together against the head wind. Mr Java is still in his pyjamas, his coat open and flapping, unshaven, hair mussed, shivering from the cold. The girls are shocked to see him standing there like that and take him by the arms, bikes and all, and push him inside . . . He stinks, his pyjamas still smell of night, his right hand is bleeding . . . What's happened? And where is Mother, for heaven's sake?

'I just needed to get some air,' says Mr Java.

Mother is in the sitting room, at the dinner table, next to the tea and biscuits, lost in a book . . . 'Oh goodness, was he really outside on the street?'

'Why isn't he dressed yet?' asks first sister.

'He wanted to sleep off his nightmare,' says Mother.

'I'm fine now,' says Mr Java, hoping to escape to the bathroom.

'First tell us what you dreamed,' says Mother, 'get it off your chest.' She slides a cup of tea towards him.

'It was about Monkey.'

'Not again!' the girls shout as one.

Mr Java is shivering, he can't hold his teacup properly. (Don't throw it, don't throw it, the boy begs silently, it's not the cup's fault.) After two spilt mouthfuls he bites his right hand – the hand calms down. 'I was so ridiculously hot . . . I was digging a very deep pit, naked.'

'Yuck!' Third sister pokes out her tongue.

'Go on,' insists Mother. He mustn't bottle up his dreams – doctor's orders. They're nasty substances, like pee or poo.

'All right,' Mr Java snaps, 'just let me dig . . .'

Blood drips on the floor. The girls shudder. 'Mummy, why didn't you do something?'

'I can't keep my eye on him all day, he hides from me.' She walks out of the room to get the iodine.

'This is . . . just look . . . he's covered in it!' The girls are lost for words.

'My mother was standing next to me,' Mr Java says, grimacing with pain as the drops of iodine soak into the wound. 'In our garden.'

'That must have been nice,' first sister soothes.

'Not at all . . . Monkey was up in the tree. And I was naked in front of my mother . . . it was horrible.'

Mother and the girls look at him pityingly. In his thoughts the boy leafs through the photo album, trying to picture the garden and Monkey and a grand-mother who stayed there . . . he doesn't dare to think of nakedness.

Mr Java tries to tell the rest of his dream, digging and digging; no one can make head nor tail of it. '"Monkey's a thief," my mother said, "he'll dig up the whole garden."' Mr Java holds out his hands, his nails are dirty . . . from digging. How is that possible, he had a bath last night before he went to bed! And that wound on his hand, how did he get that?

'A blister from a shovel,' Mr Java says. 'Headpower.' The boy chokes on his tea. 'I materialised the blister . . . If you think hard enough about something, it becomes real.' Mr Java studies his nails.

There is a long silence. The boy looks at Mother and the girls out of the corner of his eye, he can see them thinking, concentrated and keen: about record players, new bikes, and paper-hangers at work on the dinette . . .

'Have you started that new medication?' Mother asks at last.

'That's what's causing it,' says Mr Java.

'It's supposed to relax you.'

'I'm very relaxed, yes? I sleep all day.'

The boy thinks of his lost shoe . . . harder than hard, he can feel it . . . almost . . . But the miracle of materialisation eludes him.

behind the curtain 2

'The whole village knows by now,' says middle sister.

'Careful, there's no telling where he'll pop up next,' whispers first sister.

'He's a laughing stock.'

'Poor mad Horse-Man.'

'They're scared of him.'

'He's already packed his bag.'

'Mummy's ready.'

'And that kid . . . it's not right, he believes all that rubbish.'

'Mummy's going to talk to his teacher about it.'

the flood

Sunday, dustday. The boy is sitting under the table rubbing the ball legs. Mr Java is standing at the window listening to the radio. *Shhhhh*. The radio news service with a special bulletin! A spring tide has ravaged the country in the night ... The dikes have burst. Large areas of Zeeland, South Holland and West Brabant have been inundated. Correspondents report chaos and panic, dead sheep and cattle are floating in the fields and the farmers refuse to evacuate ... Army and navy are on the way ... A woman has given birth on a raft ... Waders and oilskins crackle over the radio.

A natural disaster, and Mr Java hasn't noticed a thing. Even though he used to announce high-water days in advance! (Tipped off by the lifeboat horses.) Those bloody tablets ... Apparently Mother had to go out in the night to bolt a rattling shutter and the sand from the dunes has blown into the far corners of the hall. But the horses, why didn't they –

'Duiveland has completely disappeared,' screams a radio voice from a helicopter. Dozens of people have drowned. The dike burst in Willemstad, near Fort

Sabina, the caretaker drowned. 'Call your mother,' says Mr Java between two of the reporter's sentences. He's got the atlas down from the bookcase and moved a chair in front of the radio, 'Half her family's been flooded.'

The farmers are up on their roofs. Dead horses float over drowned streets.

Mother rushes into the room with uncombed hair and together they point out the flooded areas in the atlas. The girls have already gone outside for a look: the sand is two feet high against the back door. They whoop and jump next to the radio – the dunes have been breached, the sea has come in as far as the climbing dune. 'We could have drowned.'

And not a dog barked, not a horse whinnied . . .

Mr Java is not listening any more, he's already in the hall with a coat on over his pyjamas. 'I have to check the horses.'

'It's almost enough to drive you back to God,' says Mother. She sits down in front of the radio and searches for more news, but the other station is singing unsuspecting hymns. 'Damn,' she says, 'I'll ring them up.' And she too pulls on a coat without stopping to wash.

The boy is left behind at the table with the girls. They spread extra butter on their Sunday zwieback and look out at the grey spatters on the front window – salt, the sea is biting into the glass. Across the road the storm is dangling from the tops of the pines – a piece of canvas, peeled branches . . . and what's that orange thing?

'A sou'wester,' says first sister with an expert eye.

'How'd it get there?' asks middle sister.

'From a lifeboat.'

'And our Horse-Man slept through it all,' they snigger.

'How many people drowned?' asks third sister.

'Hundreds . . .'

'And thousands of cows and horses and pigs.'

'Tomorrow the carcasses will wash up here.'

The boy sneezes on his zwieback.

—

Mr Java and Mother come back in together. They look relieved, even though their coats are white with sand. Grandfather hasn't been washed away and the horses are safe in the stable. 'Up to their hoofs in sand,' says Mr Java, 'we've got some sweeping to do.'

The milkman let Mother use his phone. The tenant's flooded, and so are loads of aunts and uncles, but no one drowned. 'Grandpa has taken in Marie from behind the church, and Uncle Leonard with the goat is coming too.' Her voice sounds higher . . . her vowels sing – suddenly she's speaking with a West Brabant accent.

'I should have known, yes?' says Mr Java. 'The horses have been restless for days . . . of course, *they* sensed it, yes?' Out of solidarity he greases his East Indian satay accent with a few extra *yeses*.

'It's all because of the hydrogen bomb,' says Mother. 'This is nature's revenge.'

'Rubbish, you and your bomb, yes?'

'And you and your horses.'

Yes, the bomb. No, the bomb. The spring flood slips under the table and they cheerfully get back to war.

Until the following afternoon when the paper issues a special edition and the damp news trembles in Mr Java's hands: at least one hundred and fifty dead. After an excited day at school (drawing and reading out loud all day), the boy studies the newspaper over Mr Java's shoulder. **In-un-dat-ed** it says in bold letters – a word for his exercise book. He asks for the photo of a pilot who saved farmers, but doesn't get it; on the other side of the page there's a picture of a pile of drowned animals. No, Mr Java couldn't say it out loud, no . . . but maybe that was even worse, all those dumb animals.

One glance is enough to send Mother rushing back to the milkman. Before dinnertime she's found out how all of her cousins are doing and what they need, and she's telephoned Aunt Mina, who lives above it all and is stingy and rich . . . Yes, even she is going to do something for her stricken relatives. She's already put aside an old fur coat.

There's a map of the disaster area in the newspaper: black is water; white, 'unflooded'. When everyone has finished the paper, the boy is finally allowed to trace the map. He makes the white parts black as well. Later he feels guilty and adds a raft, an outrigger proa, a steamboat with three smoking cigars and as many bearers as he can fit in the margins.

—

Mother spends the next day running back and forth between home and telephone as well: Grandfather rode a motorbike over the dike next to his land, the water was up at least twenty feet, he saw cows floating on both sides. The mayor of Klundert is missing and the army has appointed a student in his place — for twenty-four hours! The tenant spent eighteen hours in a rowing boat with his wife and child . . . and Grandfather's cleaning woman spent two nights in her attic, the sea had smashed in through the windows and she could hear the dressing table pounding on the ceiling . . . Three days on the phone and Mother knows more than the radio!

Mr Java drowses his hours at the hotel reading table . . . he'd like to take a draught horse to Zeeland, rescue livestock or drive a jeep or a motorboat . . . he used to be able to do all those things, but the only thing he does now is blacken his hands on piles of newspapers. He even neglects his lifeboat horses.

At home the newspaper on the mat incites its readers to action: 'Help is needed: money, blankets, toys. Soldiers and students – volunteer now!' Mother wants to do something. She owes it to her family: when she arrived in the Netherlands robbed and destitute they did so much for her . . . But what can she do? A lady on the dune sent her char to Zeeland to shovel mud, that was a nice gesture. But Mr Java can't get by without her, he's been so sleepy the last few days, maybe the girls . . . They'd jump at the chance, but they're more useful on dry ground. She'll send her cousins a bag of clothes. And the girls can go collecting; the art teacher drew a picture of a drowned horse on the board and they made postcards of it, they can sell them door to door for twenty-five cents each.

The boy wants to help too. He drags the bag of clothes. Mother does a round of the wardrobes. Mr Java can easily miss a few shirts. And shoes? She peeks into the hall to make sure the coast is clear . . . and carefully opens (with a finger on her lips, this is her and the boy's secret) Mr Java's creaking chest of drawers. A pair of fur-lined Bally ankle boots slide into the bottom of the bag. Under one of her reform dresses. The girls give up two prickly pullovers between them – once received themselves and now passed on generously. And him?

The jacket!

'No.'

'You hardly wear it.'

'It's my favourite.'

'The other day you said, "I'd rather wear my old coat."'

'To keep my new one new.'

'Pull the other one, why don't you?' Mother takes the jacket from the coat hook but the boy clamps his fists around the bag. 'Don't you want to make one of your poor cousins happy?'

But the boy sticks to his guns: what's a country bumpkin want with his jacket? If she gives it away, he'll have nothing left.

'Open it,' Mother orders. She tugs at the bag. The boy resists – he finds a pilot's courage – he fights for his jacket, fists closed like iron, he kicks out, he bites her hand. Mother hits back. The girls come to her rescue. They're always ready for a fight. They strangle the boy and stuff the jacket into the bag. Mr Java doesn't do a thing, he stares silently at the postcard of the drowned horse. Not like the women! They roll up their sleeves, especially in emergencies.

Mother says, 'You only think of yourself.'

medal day

Mr Java is polishing his medals. He found them while tidying up, in a black tin. Now they're spread out on an old newspaper. Brasso, sand, lemon, Vim and an old woollen sock are there to buff up his heroic deeds. Mr Java has pulled out the certificates that accompanied the medals, to read off his achievements: 'Royal Decree No. 26. The silver medal for proven valour to the Instructor of Cavalry . . .' He growls. 'Nonsense. We were so brave we shat ourselves. They never told us what it would be like, so . . . um, complicated.' Mr Java is thinking out loud. '. . . Complicated, yes, serving a country you don't know, a country that disowns you . . . in a country *they* don't know. Fighting for strangers, *against* people you know. Reaping by destroying crops . . . being praised for your deeds, regretting what you've done and wanting to do it again tomorrow.'

Middle sister acts as if she hasn't heard; she's half watching, her other half is reading. The boy listens open-mouthed.

'They've crossed out Colonies,' says Mr Java, who is shocked by his own voice. He tries to conceal his uneasiness by going through the certificate as if it's a dictation: 'Presented as a token of appreciation by HRH . . . with capitals and dots . . . it's an old certificate but they've updated it by typing Ministry of Overseas Territories at the top. Overseas . . . Over sighs.' He shines up a bronze queen and uses a sharpened match to pick the dirt out of her crown. 'Sorry, ma'am, we did it for you. For Queen and Country . . . But don't believe anyone who tells you they think about the queen when they're wading through mud up to their waist.'

'Why haven't you got any gold medals?' middle sister interrupts.

'Gold is for officers,' mumbles Mr Java.

'Weren't you promoted?'

'I couldn't go any higher . . . we couldn't afford the school.'

'But you were so rich?'

'Not then. My father died and my mother put us in an orphanage because it was easier to look for a new husband without children.'

'And when she found him?'

'Mobilisation started and I was fully qualified . . .'

'As what?'

'A cleaner.' Mr Java turns over the bronze medal and starts on the back.

'E ... va ... por ...' the boy spells upside down from the back of the medal.

Pro valore.

out of pocket

Fine, he fought heroically for his country – the whole bloody village knows that – to the bitter end: beyond the ocean and past the deserts, where the globe is welded together, smack on the equator. On horseback, paddling in a proa, dangling from the talons of an eagle – in a manner of speaking at least. He endured danger. Real danger. Bullets, shells, ambushes, volcanic eruptions . . . he was spared nothing. And what did he end up with? Scars, medals and a small pension.

'It's not a pension,' Mother corrects him. 'You won't get that till much later.'

'But I have a right.'

'For now you get benefits.'

'I'm not benefiting from anything!'

'Call it indemnification.'

'Indemnification . . . damnification, more like! I have to go down on my knees before those people.' Mr Java claps his hands over his eyes and growls like a

94

wolf. He hates the language of bureaucracy. 'A pittance is what it is, a lousy pittance!'

But all of a sudden he's not getting anything any more, not these last two months. The envelopes from the Postal Cheque and Giro Service have stopped coming. He's written, called, spent hours standing at windows, but the ladies and gentlemen of the accounts department don't give a peep and the local council is even worse. Mr Java is no longer listed. Gone. Swallowed up. No name, no address. Past or present, they don't know a thing. Had he ever actually registered? And how long has he been in the country? No one understands it. No matter how Mr Java implores them, despite all the proofs he's shown – medals, proud flesh on calf and upper arm, traces of bullet, whip and barbed wire – it leaves them cold. First he has to prove he exists. Fill in the questionnaire in triplicate and submit it by registered mail.

Mother helps him when she can: she even put on a suit to go and beg the Royal Commissioner. She looks invincible, with a cardboard bust, someone to cross the road to avoid . . . but she didn't get further than the county hall waiting room. 'This whole country is one big waiting room,' sighs Mr Java.

The girls sympathise, the boy is more obedient than ever and quietly practises Mr Java's handwriting on the used sheets of carbon paper . . . Pension, pension, it's a word he must have heard in the cradle. The girls know what's expected of them in life: choose a profession with a pension. Neighbours and visitors talk about it: who is offering the best pension? Unfortunately, the hand is deaf to what the ear hears often: *Penshun, penshen, penshoon* . . . The word just won't turn out on paper.

—

As soon as the boy has got the spelling down pat, he will write a faultless plea to the queen.

The civil servants come up with the weirdest ways of searching for Mr Java. After the questionnaires, he has to go in for a medical as well. A medical! As if he has something to hide. Bandy legs, yes, because he learnt to ride before he could walk. Or is that forbidden now as well? Is he supposed to be ashamed of himself because his father wasn't a worker? Mr Java rails against the world. But he knows: being obstructive won't get him anywhere, so he sighs in front of the window, swears under his breath, crushes a geranium in his fist and submits to the whims of officialdom.

They send him to a clinic in the city for the medical. They want to count his bones and the fillings in his teeth. Gold, not lead! That means extra teeth-brushing, an extended bath, talcum on his bottom, his best underwear, garters and suit. Not sackcloth, his best tweed. He drags the boy along with him – let them damn well see he's brought a child into the world who needs his care. 'Come on, into your Sunday best.

We'll show 'em. We're no cadgers. We've got our rights and we're sticking up for them.'

Outside the building, Mr Java takes off his overcoat and hands it to his son. Then he empties the pockets of his suit . . . wallet, lighter, letter of notification, a handkerchief, a lost twenty-five cents . . . 'Here, son, put it out of sight.' And now he turns all of his pockets inside-out. Coat pockets, trouser pockets – side, inside and back. Two white points stick out from his hips, two from his side, two at the back. A small twist, controlled and dignified . . . one last tug left and right on the points of the white lining and Mr Java rings the bell: solemnly penniless. He strolls in with his head held high. The boy follows, weighed down by the overcoat. Doorman, nurses, doctors . . . they all recoil.

Mr Java has grown wings.

Aunt Mina

A black limo is parked in front of the house. Sitting behind the wheel is Pete, Aunt Mina's servant, gardener and chauffeur; his cap is pushed up against the windscreen above the dashboard and looks like two caps, one of glass and one of cloth. Pete's trying to soak up a little sun, he leans back to smoke and flicks his ash out of the driver's window. Pete's not allowed inside. Aunt Mina is on a tour of inspection. She's come to assess the flood damage: never mind that these particular relatives haven't suffered any, she carries out an inspection every year, preferably unannounced on a Sunday so she can go to church with the whole family afterwards, but this time she informed them of her arrival twenty-four hours in advance – enough time to get her gifts out of the cupboards and display them prominently.

Like Mother, Aunt Mina is from a farming family, but because she married a notary she is the richest of all. She has left the manure far behind her and lives in a mansion. 'We'd be lost without her,' Mother says, and when she's at her wits' end, she sometimes calls her (Mr Java mustn't know). Aunt Mina has promised each of the girls a case of silverware if they marry in church. She doesn't have any children of her own and when she dies, Mother will inherit one hundred and fifty acres. (Behind her back they've already spent the money dozens of times: a car and, if possible, a house of their own. 'So we can stop sharing the hall with all these deadbeats,' says Mr Java. Mother wants to live higher, somewhere hilly, beyond the reach of spring tides and with a deep cellar to keep out the fallout. 'Somewhere respectable,' Mr Java agrees.)

There is nothing Aunt Mina would rather see than the family coming back up in the world. She finds it hard to accept that her niece went to the colonies so young and became alienated from her family in Zeeland. To prove the contrary, Mother is wearing her traditional gold earrings and has polished the silver clasps on the family Bible. The girls have been given strict instructions: skirts below the knee and film stars off the wall; the boy has to show his school exercise book – with clean nails, please. 'And watch your tongue: no "goshing" or "geeing." Aunt Mina hears curses in everything.' Mr Java has taken a new tablet, shaken out of a tube by Mother herself and laid beside the custard. After her last visit, Mina complained about him, he was too touchy by half. This time will be better. There's an inheritance at stake . . .

'Still no job?' she asks over the first cup of coffee. Her double chin quivers, her voice grates, she's used to giving orders.

Mr Java shows her his correspondence folder. 'It's coming, it's coming.' He feigns servility, but his hands are trembling with rage.

'I'm sure.'

'I have hundreds of applications pending.'

'Easy does it, relax.'

'It will pay off in the end.'

'How long have you been out of work?'

'I'm not stupid enough.'

'Of course not.' She pulls the folder over, looking at Mother out of the corner of her eye. She puts on her gold glasses and ruffles through the clipped-out advertisements and rejection letters. *Town clerk's office, administrator, administrative staff* . . . 'Why only clerical? You've got two hands, haven't you?'

Mr Java grinds his smile.

'And what's this?' She holds up a certificate: *Gratitude of Her Majesty the Queen.* 'Goodness!' There's a coupon stuck to the back. *C&A Brenninkmeijer. Men's Wear, General Fashion. Valid for one pair of trousers.* 'It's expired,' says Aunt Mina.

'I don't shop at C&A.'

'Shop? You only had to pick it up!'

'It's poor quality.'

Aunt Mina turns to Mother and the girls (who are drinking coffee with their knees together) and says, 'Listen who's giving himself airs.'

———

At the table. Set stylishly with damask. Owing to the seriousness of the occasion, the family is eating a hot meal in the middle of the day, like farmers – but modest. Omelette and cauliflower with potatoes and a second tablet for Mr Java. He's gone as white as the sauce. Aunt Mina reads from the Bible over the steam. Then she waits for grace with fingers drumming. The girls rattle it off in chorus.

'I didn't hear your brother,' says Aunt Mina. 'Again, and just him this time.'

'Bless these blessed gifts, oh Lord, amen.' That's all he knows.

'Who taught you that?'

Mother looks over her clasped hands at Mr Java. 'But at school he's very precocious,' she says. 'Show Aunt Mina your exercise book.'

The boy is sitting on his exercise book – proudly, he knows that Aunt Mina gives money when she's in a good mood, tiny folded-up notes – but he hesitates . . .

'Go on, give it to her,' Mother gestures impatiently. 'He could already read and write before he went to school,' she tells Aunt Mina. Mr Java hangs over the cauliflower with his eyes screwed shut, his hands still locked together from the prayer.

First sister takes charge at the table, cutting the omelette. Middle sister walks around the table to dish it out. The boy gets the smallest piece. 'Too much is bad for your hives.' His allergy is a matter of general concern.

'Don't you trust your Aunt Mina?' first sister teases.

The boy fidgets on his chair.

'Sit still,' Mother snaps.

Middle sister pokes him and first sister snatches the exercise book out from under his bottom. Aunt Mina is already holding out her hand. 'Here you are,' says first sister with a courtly nod.

Aunt Mina leafs through it, she giggles, her eyebrows jiggle above her glasses. 'What's it say here?' She holds the exercise book at an angle for first sister.

'Undination,' says first sister.

'And here?'

'Cave . . . caveuation . . . prings foold.'

Mother jumps up and reaches for the exercise book, third sister wants to look too, first sister holds it up high and leafs through the pages: drawings, maps, sums, sentences, traced letters and words flutter over the table. With a shriek, middle sister points to a picture that's been printed from the newspaper. 'And this is a . . .' She looks more closely at the enormous letters underneath it, as if she can't believe her eyes . . . 'A jet gifter pliot.' She presses her lips together.

'What's a jet gifter pliot?'

'I mean a jet fighter pilot,' the boy says.

The girls burst out laughing. They can't help themselves. Mother doesn't laugh, she roars . . . from nerves. The omelette is stuck in the back of her throat.

Mr Java wakes up from his prayer. 'To your room,' he drawls.

—

The boy lies down on his bed and hides the exercise book under his mattress . . . no one will look there. That's where he keeps the flat cigar box full of bullets he found in the dunes, with beautiful sharp points, from a Kraut carbine. He holds one up against his ear: a jet fighter roars in the storm. Mr Java knocks on the door, he steps into the room . . . the boy quickly hides the bullet in his fist. 'They didn't mean it like that,' Mr Java says, 'Aunt Mina is just . . .'

'Mean.'

'She's a Calvinist.'

The boy doesn't have to come back to the table, he can take a bowl of soup out to Pete. 'Why doesn't he eat with us?'

'Pete prefers to stay in the car.'

As he walks to the car, the bullet tingles in the bottom of his trouser pocket, the spoon tinkles in the bowl . . . He sees himself approaching in the polished black metal like in a fairground mirror, wide and small; the bowl turns into a soup tureen . . . But the strange, fat mirror boy isn't laughing, he prays that he won't spill the soup and thinks of the bullet in his pocket, a furious bullet that wants to scratch . . . a long line over the boot, unnoticed in passing . . . a jet fighter track.

Pete stubs out his cigarette and winds down the window. The smoke mingles with the steam from the soup, a pair of gnarled hands take the bowl . . . a nod, a gap-toothed grin . . . So this is a servant, the first one the boy has ever seen, a chauffeur who's not allowed in the house, with hands like trays and a ribcage of twisted roots.

'You's a good lad,' says Pete.

The bullet shrinks in the boy's pocket.

—

Before leaving, Aunt Mina takes Mother aside in the sitting room for a moment: she wants to go through the housekeeping book. The girls have already been rewarded; the sharply folded ten-guilder notes were pressed into their hands and now they're in the bedroom ironing their spoils. Mr Java and the boy were sent into the hall without a cent. The door closes behind them, but aunt's voice carries through the walls. 'And that medicine,' they hear her asking, 'doesn't the health service pay for that?'

'Nerves aren't covered.'

'And the benefit cut as well.'

'It must be a mistake,' says Mother.

'The cake's not made of elastic . . .'

'He's got so many problems from the . . .' Mother whispers something. Mr Java and the boy keep quiet behind the door . . . his heel scratches a circle in the lino.

'He looks perfectly . . .'

'. . .'

'Camp? Oh, you mean the war!' Aunt Mina screeches through the room. 'Don't get me started!'

'No,' Mother says quietly.

'A terrible time . . . five years of eating hare!'

thieving fingers

Aunt Mina gave Mother a box of cherry liqueurs as a gift. The boy has never seen letters as beautiful as the ones on that box. Curly raised-up letters of thick gold, even a blind man could read them, perfect for tracing. Unfortunately, not his to practise on. Mother keeps it in the top of the cupboard to open on a festive occasion, but that's not likely to be any time soon.

A month later the box is still in the cupboard. Up on a chair to have a look, tracing the letters – the wavy CH, the manufacturer's signature – and feeling them, of course: five red cherries on green stems, the veins in the leaves, the smooth cellophane. But it's not just the outside of the box that's enticing, inside it's rustling . . .

He's already held it to his ear to listen to how many are inside. Before putting the box away again. For days now. Until the nail of his little finger cautiously explores the edge of the cellophane and slips in without tearing it. The lid is sucked tight, pop, chocolate wafts out – there's no way back. Under blankets of gleaming brown paper, two dozen chocolates in corrugated tubs long for a greedy mouth. The boy takes out two, rearranging the remaining twenty-two and tucking them back in. Lid on, fold back the cellophane, a lick of gum arabic along the edge and no one will be any the wiser. The next day he takes another two, and the following day, two more. He's more cunning than he thought. He builds a honeycomb of empty tubs. With his thieving fingers.

Weeks later Mother gets the chocolates down from the cupboard and opens an empty box . . . The whole family is called in. Inspect, sniff . . . That's right, it was wrapped tight in cellophane, the tubs are intact . . . strange, it must be a manufacturing error! The family won't stand for it. Mr Java immediately sits down at the table to write an angry letter to the manager of the chocolate factory. Mother and the girls lean over his shoulder to read along. 'Dear Sir . . . You supplied us with one pound of air. An empty façade! Potemkin chocolates. Whatever happened to the pride of craftsmanship? Do the workers still see the final product?'

Mr Java screws up one sheet after the other, he is not at his best, he can't find the right tone . . . '"No one in this country does a proper job any more!" Shall I finish with that?'

'Maybe not,' says Mother.

'But things like this never used to happen here.'

'How would you know?'

Mr Java snorts, 'It's the socialists' fault, Holland is going to the dogs.' Yes, that will be the last sentence.

The boy shares their indignation, but is mostly struck by how strange it is that people who have known hunger can leave their sweets in the top of a cupboard for so long.

on the train

Mr Java has an appointment in town with a lawyer. Mother wants the boy to go with him so she'll have less to worry about – lately Mr Java has been getting into all kinds of trouble. They'll have to take the local and change on the way. And the boy will have to take a day off school. It's about something that's been dragging on for ever, but that's all Mother was willing to say.

'What's a lawyer do?' the boy asks on the way to the train station.

'Helps dishonest people,' Mr Java mumbles, lost in thought. At the ticket office he buys two returns, one second class and one third class. Third class for the boy, second class for himself. That's as much frugality as Mr Java can muster. The third-class people are crammed in too close together, third-class seats are too hard for his heart, third class stinks of rancid flannels, third class . . . he stumbles over his own excuses, but the boy is too astonished to object. He sneezes.

'You're never too young to learn to travel alone,' Mr

Java says, leaving the boy on the third-class step. 'We'll see each other soon at the big station.'

—

The boy finds a window seat. The glass is slightly reflective, if he sits at a certain angle he can see two things at once: the landscape and his own head. The train moves off and he sees his face flashing over the bank. Fifteen minutes later the train cuts through a meadow and cows are grazing in his hair. Along the canal it's less exciting, dark and empty, a dull section he remembers from other trips (second class), but after a slight curve a different glitter appears on the water . . . half the compartment is reflected in the window. The boy wipes the corners of his mouth, tucks his springy shirt collar back in under the neck of his pullover . . . chin up . . . yes, that makes him look tidier. He looks at himself the way he thinks others see him: a boy alone on a train. A brave little fellow. Where could he be going? And why doesn't he have any bags with him? Surely he's not running away? Travelling without a father, without a mother . . . maybe he's a war orphan. From a good family, you see that at a glance: beautiful, long, grey flannel trousers with turn-ups, a pullover without any stains, in perfect condition. And such shiny shoes! He's got clean nails as well, no writer's bump, maybe the start of one . . . Why does he keep looking in the pocket of his trousers? Sit still for a change! He's certainly acting strangely, surely he doesn't have something to hide? There goes that hand again. Yes, he's fiddling with something . . . surely not? Hey, kid, what are you doing in that pocket? What are you hiding? A hankie . . . And under it? A tightly folded ten-guilder note in the bottom corner of the pocket. Why is it buried so deep . . . come on, tell us that? Because it's stolen money – from the housekeeping purse. It just happened, his thieving fingers took it before he knew it. There was no voice telling him not to. But now his eyes betray him. And his soft, flaccid lips. The man opposite is watching him . . . he too looks out, their eyes meet in the reflective window. The man smiles at him, he's laughing at him . . . he looks straight through him . . . that's what it feels like . . . naked. Beautiful pullover, expensive trousers, all true – but the man knows: inside he's a common thief. A cheat. The boy tries to look the other way, unable to face even himself.

The train glides into a curve, the sun seems to turn with it, and the window and canal stop reflecting . . . his thieving face vanishes. The meadows come closer again. And the boy sees nothing but cows. He fidgets. Not daring to look at the man across from him, he makes trails in the soft material of his trousers and plays with the lid of the ashtray.

The local train stops at every station and slows down for Rosehill, the loony bin. Sometimes the loonies throw themselves in front of the train, the girls told him that. He presses his nose up against the glass to look at the gravel alongside the tracks. Nothing to

111

see. The chocolate factory is smoking away, the carriages plough through cocoa fumes. The boy spells the word on the glass with a finger: *coaco . . . cocao*.

Even larger factories and chimneys whizz by. The compartment gets more crowded. New passengers board, carrying in the smells of the factories: linoleum, coffee, flour, fresh-sawn wood. Men in corduroy trousers, women in aprons . . . he breathes in their clothing. This is what third class smells like. And it doesn't even make him sneeze. When the train moves off again, the man opposite him slumps down on his seat, his knee touches the boy's flannel. The boy presses back, the knee slides forward . . . A woman comes and sits next to the man. The knee withdraws and the boy takes refuge in the creases of his trousers . . . until his eyes wander again and he sees a pale, flabby man on the other side of the corridor. The man waves. At him! He's still wearing his mittens. 'Hello, sir,' the boy replies softly. He hadn't noticed him before, maybe he just got on. Those enormous mittens look ridiculous. In this spring weather.

The boy tries to think of something else. But he can't keep his eyes off those mittens. He has to look, just as he has to sniff up the sweaty smell from the knee opposite – his nose and eyes make him.

The fat man keeps waving. A loony, thinks the boy, an escaped nutcase. He waves back – he doesn't want to, he has no choice!

There's a friend, thinks the loony, a friend who's saying hello . . . I'll shake his hand! The lunatic takes his right mitten between his teeth and pulls it off to expose his fingers. A white hand flutters over the corridor. Can the boy believe his eyes? A white hand with six fingers! Long, wobbly fingers.

The woman diagonally opposite picks up her bag and walks off. The boy nervously checks that the stolen money is still in his pocket. The dirty knee creeps closer to the flannel trousers. The six-fingered hand sees its chance and slides over to the empty spot. The knee jumps . . . The boy's eyes clamp on to the six fingers. It's a flower waving there . . . a white sea anemone. A strange excitement takes charge of the boy: the hand is so clean, so baby soft . . . Unemployed. Fingers with no history. A divine miscount, but free of sin. More innocent than his own, thieving fingers.

These then are the third-class people, with their third-class manners and their third-class smells. And he is even lower.

—

It's busy at the big station. Hats, bags, suitcases and bellowing porters force their way through the travellers. The boy panics when he can't see Mr Java among the other people getting off the train but a second later he is fished out of the mob by his collar. Mr Java holds him tight but doesn't look at him, he's

113

busy talking to a blonde lady. Where has she suddenly come from? She's wearing a long, light-blue coat, immaculately second class, and smells overwhelmingly of sweets and perfumed soap; her hair is shiny, just like her lips, orange lips, and she's smiling ... she's smiling at Mr Java, but she hardly notices the boy. She picks a bit of fluff off Mr Java's coat, wipes an orange smudge from his cheek ... The boy looks up at her, admiring her mother-of-pearl buttons ... When she beckons a porter and walks away to show him her suitcases, Mr Java whispers quickly in his ear, 'I'm your uncle.'

'Why?'

'Doesn't matter, call me uncle.' Uncle. Mr Java squeezes the word into his neck.

The woman comes back, followed by a trolley with suitcases. Mr Java walks her to the taxis. They have a lot to talk about ... In the underpass, their voices echo off other voices. 'Do you remember? I still have them.' The trolley wheels grind through their words. 'Why didn't you ever ... Surely you ... It could have been so wonderful ... See you, then. See you.' A goodbye kiss – on her lips – the click of high heels ... and the unknown lady disappears between the black cars in a swirl of blue. The boy didn't get a chance to say uncle.

'Who was that?'

'Oh, an acquaintance . . . I've forgotten her name,' Mr Java says absently.

An acquaintance from the old days . . . the boy has already grasped that much. Someone from the brown photos, from the country before he was born.

'Come on, we've got a few minutes.' Mr Java pushes the boy to the granite steps and they hurry side by side to the express. 'And now we'll get a breath of fresh air,' Mr Java says, steering the boy into the gangway between second and third class, there where two carriages are joined together, where it blows and steams and hisses, where two iron tongues slide over each other, light glitters through the chinks and you can see the rails gleaming under your feet. 'In the old days, when I was a kid, I'd pat the elephants here,' says Mr Java. 'Back then they used to make the passage between the carriages from elephant skin. Harmonicas that could withstand almost anything. Half an inch thick, a normal hunting rifle wouldn't penetrate it. If only our skins were that thick . . .'

The train starts moving. Mr Java and the boy stand on their own metal plates and hold each other tight. They wobble, shake . . . 'Eyes shut,' Mr Java shouts over the *kerchunk, kerchunk* between second and third.

The boy takes a deep breath and lets the wind catch his face. His eyes water. He feels a splash on his cheek – a tear from Mr Java. 'Let it flow, son, the dirt has to come out.'

The money is burning in his pocket, the boy kneads it into a ball and drops it between the two iron tongues in the middle of a screeching curve . . . the wind gobbles it up. Mr Java doesn't notice, he's floating through his memories with eyes shut. But the boy doesn't want to remember. He wants to forget that he's a thief. To forget everything. The dirt has to come out.

betrayal

When he arrives home, Mr Java's whole body is shaking. Mother can't believe her eyes. The boy is shaking as well. His hair is a mess, there are lines of snot on his pullover. But Mr Java is worse: tie crooked, suit dirty and grey from . . . yes, from what? What happened? And why are they so late? It's already dinnertime, the girls are sitting round the table.

'Betrayal. Pure and simple. It's enough to make your blood boil!' Mr Java rages over a hurriedly dished up plate of macaroni. 'How informative a visit to a lawyer can be.'

'Maybe we should discuss it later,' Mother says soothingly, 'when you've calmed down a little.'

But Mr Java's rage will tolerate no postponement. He doesn't care who knows, the whole table, the whole village, the whole country, that he, Mr Java – unemployed and on the dole (yes, let's say it out loud for once) – drinks two cups of coffee every day in the most expensive hotel in the village, served in a silver pot with three biscuits on a saucer, so that he can then spend hours reading a pile of newspapers and magazines, national and foreign, for the sum of one guilder a day. Cheaper than a subscription. And that is why his benefits have been cut off. Because the council is scared that the unemployed might all start spending their time sipping coffee in posh hotels, and how could one explain that? One doesn't pay one's taxes to support that kind of behaviour.

One, one . . . The word disgusts Mr Java. Who removed him from the card index?

One!

On the sly.

It's a disgrace. Even the girls are on his side. Briefly, because when he tells them that he slammed the lawyer's door so hard it brought down the portrait of the queen – smashed to pieces – and how he and the boy then raced to the town hall, where they arrived just in time to drag a civil servant over the counter, first sister mutters, 'That's not the way one should act.'

'I'm no *one*!' Mr Java screeches over the table. Under his chin his tie flaps with excitement. The girls freeze behind their plates and Mother quickly dissolves a tablet in some water. Mr Java knocks the glass out of her hands – no more medicine, he's had enough of being coddled and caged.

'You're out of control!' says Mother.

'And rude,' say the girls.

'You starting now as well?' Don't worry, Mr Java can scream even louder. They should have seen him this afternoon, with that cowardly civil servant. But that's how he found out who betrayed him . . . He falls silent and looks at them expectantly. No one asks, 'Who?' 'Mrs Bentinck,' he says at last.

'Mrs Bentinck?' the dining table cries.

Yes, that lady who's eternally collecting for all known diseases, the champion of all that is virtuous, the woman who fills the local rag with weepy, bleeding-heart articles, which he himself from pure goodness has even read, yes, Mrs Bentinck, with her pony, that insult to horse- and womankind alike, the one who always sings on her bike and rings her bell – here I come – who's always so cute and laconic, with her mouth full of opinions, yes, *she* reported him . . . *She* betrayed him.

'And you know what I did then, yes?' Two fists rest on the sides of his plate . . . the macaroni trembles.

'You go too far,' Mother warns.

No, Mr Java is only just getting started: he gave Mrs Bentinck a piece of his mind. When she came riding by this afternoon, in the village! He just stopped her and held her front wheel jammed against the gutter with his foot . . . She hadn't done any harm, she said. She just happened to mention it to a civil servant,

119

she said. No, she hadn't written any letters, SHE LIED! Mr Java screams . . . and whimpers and whines.

The girls hold hands under the table, squeezing each other calm. Mother stirs her macaroni to mash. And the boy? He's not there. He's sitting there, but he's practising not being there, with all the headpower he can muster.

'That bike can go straight to the tip,' says Mr Java.

'Mrs Bentinck's?' the girls ask anxiously.

'Stamped it underfoot.' To emphasise his words Mr Java brings his fists down on the sides of his plate, the macaroni splashes in his face. Surprised, he stares at the mess he's made.

The dinner table freezes – but not for long, dinner's getting cold.

'You're a disgrace to the family,' says middle sister.

Mother keeps her eyes on the boy while chewing silently. 'Weren't you with him all day?'

The boy doesn't know where to look but is determined to keep his mouth shut.

'Coward,' the girls say.

—

The girls mop the sitting room, the boy washes the wallpaper. Mother tends to Mr Java with a hot tea towel and in that silent cleaning that wipes away everything – the stains, the shards, the fury and the words – they suddenly hear a female voice singing cheerfully in the street and a shrill bicycle bell and when Mother glances out over the geraniums, she sees Mrs Bentinck whizz past – upright, in high spirits and unharmed. How is it possible?

'You think I loathe her, don't you?' says Mr Java while Mother scrubs his cuff. 'I don't, I only loathe myself, because I didn't do anything . . . didn't curse her, didn't touch a hair on her head, ab-so-lute-ly nothing.'

The girls rush up to him, tugging at his coat, pounding him on the back, 'Liar, liar.' Oh, he gave them such a fright . . . He is mad, bonkers. They'll tell the doctor everything.

Mother chases them out of the room with a tea towel. When Mr Java has tidied himself up again and is standing at the window with his hands in his pockets, sending lightning bolts after Mrs Bentinck, who has long since disappeared out of sight, he says, 'I feel like an elephant on a stool: shake hands, do a trick, take your tablets . . . But I want to go back to the jungle.'

'And then?' asks Mother.

'Tear up trees.'

'And then?'

'Trumpet loudly. Go after my enemies.'

'Who are your enemies?'

'*Turooooo* . . .' Mr Java trumpets. And when he runs out of breath, 'You don't need to tell me. I know . . . I'm a dead weight. Just send me away.'

Mother decides – a monologue

I don't know how old my mother was when she died in childbirth, I never asked or dwelt on it . . . but her dead face is something I will never forget, it's my first memory, on my father's arm.

The next day we left the farm and moved into a house in the village. We took a tenant and my father became a gentleman farmer.

Goodbyes have been easy for me ever since.

The train to Paris crossed my father's land. Paris – for a farm girl that was the other side of the world. Sometimes it stopped in the middle of the field, sighing clouds of steam. A cook with a tall white hat worked in the dining-car kitchen.

'Can I go to Paris?' I asked my father.

'You belong in the clay country,' he said.

At sixteen I climbed on to the train. Smuggled aboard by the wagons-lits cook. No time to say goodbye.

In Paris I saw men from the south, black-skinned and brown-skinned men from the deserts and the tropics: reading books in Le Métro, or at the market standing behind boxes of sun-dried fruit. When they laughed their teeth were dazzling, and on a summer's day, in the middle of the Bois de Boulogne, there was a man in a white linen suit, with an aristocratic smile. These men were nothing like the boys from my village, I can assure you of that.

'Aren't we good enough for you?' my father asked when I told him that I was going to make a long voyage to the tropics.

'It's not that,' I said, 'I want to learn to eat rice.'

Soon after I said goodbye to the potato.

I had met a young officer at the military ball, as brown as a chestnut. He had three surnames and a mother who still ate with her hands. I married him in the tropics.

We moved from island to island, from outpost to outpost, never staying anywhere longer than a year. We always found it easy to move on. We travelled like strangers under the sun.

For the whites there, my husband was too dark and our marriage too mixed; for the dark-skinned, I was too white and he was the white man's soldier. In time we also became estranged from each other.

Three daughters kept us together.

War broke out. Men and women were split up and that

was a blessing for our marriage. His truck turned off to the right, ours went left, we didn't wave.

I raised three girls behind barbed wire. Without realising it, they said goodbye to their childhood. Too young. Lots of things were happening without our being aware of them. In the very first year of the war their father was murdered. But we only heard that after peace had come. Much too late. There was no sense in saying goodbye then – the damage had already been done.

And now this man, this crazy soldier without stripes.

Two soldiers in one life is a lot for someone who doesn't like uniforms. In my previous life I was also married to a soldier and in the two lives before that as well, a warrior's wife, time after time; this is my fifth military man. I don't know what it is that keeps attracting me to soldiers . . . Not the outfit. Maybe the idea of fighting for your country?

They say you have to do the things that don't succeed in this life over in the next. Where do I keep going wrong?

My father said, 'You should have married a farmer to keep the land in the family.' Mr Java calls himself a dead weight. 'Send me away,' he says.

I have let a lot of things slip through my fingers. But this time I'm not letting go. I will serve this marriage out, because if I don't finish it, I'll have to do it over yet again.

It's not easy saying goodbye to your failings.

behind the curtain 3

The girls are singing a song from the radio, behind the curtain in the bike hall, very quietly but still audible:

'Mother gets no Horse-Man thrills.
'Cause Horse-Man only takes his pills.'

They sing it over and over, then hum it round the house.

'Hey,' Mr Java says when he hears the melody, 'don't I know that from somewhere?'

The girls crack up.

souvenir

It is Wednesday afternoon, Mother and the girls have
gone to the city, Mr Java has locked himself up in
the dark. Time to explore. The bureau hasn't been
charted properly, there must still be hidden drawers
and crevices where secret keys are stored. The keys
from the iron tropics box, the stock box and the farm
box, where great-grandmother's silver cap brooches
are hidden: treasures to buy bread during a famine
or a berth on a refugee ship . . . when worst comes
to worst. The boy knows where they keep the boxes,
under the hatch next to the stepladder (where Mr
Java will dig the fallout shelter, when he gets his
strength back), but no keys fit them . . . up till now.
The boy too wants to be ready.

The doors of the bureau creak, the drawers jam. No
matter what he opens, he doesn't find keys, only letters,
piles of letters, bulging out, typed, handwritten, airmail
envelopes and brown ones with windows. In the old
days (he too has old days), before he went to school,
he used to snatch up the post and read the sender
out loud: Rehabilitation Scheme, Grievous Monetary

Loss, Restitution Board ... exciting words he only half understands, mysterious abbreviations: VWTS, Victims of War Tracing Service; CEB, Central Evacuation Bureau. Anything he couldn't spell, he traced – tracing paper made every message twice as important. He was only allowed to look at the outside; the inside was none of his business. Forbidden fare! Not for nosy parkers and curious cats. But now he's finally got to see the letters, he's disappointed. Where are the treasure maps, the bearer bonds (good for one thousand guilders), the blood, the bullets and the dead? He wants to smell gunpowder and count doubloons, tiger's teeth, ivory ... sniff up the pepper gardens. What use are grey, typed lines full of incomprehensible words? He wants to rap his knuckles on false bottoms, open secret panels by pressing gently with a single finger ... he seeks the thrill of being a thief.

He gets the torch and shines it into the cavernous space behind the drawers; lighting up jammed papers and envelopes that have slipped through the cracks, he rakes them forward with a ruler. A meagre catch, by the looks of it: a few airmail letters and snaps of the girls, sitting on their own father's lap. Brown photos with brown babies. And a pale one of Mother in a swimming costume. He's never seen her showing so much skin, she always keeps her dress on, even on the beach. He takes the photo over to the window to look at it in the light. So this was his mother. The mother of the girls, half-naked in the tropics, before she met Mr Java. Does he know about this? Should he lay her under his plate? His fingers explore her long, bare legs, he scrapes the white corrugated edges with his nails, it tickles . . . they're sticky . . . then he tears the photo up into vicious little pieces. To see how *that* feels.

Sliding the drawers back into place, he notices a small, gold-coloured tin inside the bureau. The lid is rusted tight, there are letters stamped on it in a strange language: EMERGENCY RATION. NOT TO BE OPENED EXCEPT BY ORDER OF AN OFFICER. Mysterious. The tin itself is more forthcoming, it rattles and says, 'Steal me.'

Thief pushes the edge of the tin against a brick wall outside. He wriggles and presses until the lid flies open. A wooden picture falls to the ground – it looks like a bit of peel, hard and round, with a hole in it. There's a drawing on it, a child's head in white and brown. Who could it be? It's only a baby, with eyes closed. One of the girls? Or the little brother who only lives in whispers . . . and if you ask, never existed.

The tin gives no answer. The lid is twisted, it can't go back into the bureau like that. He'll bury it on the dune with the shredded photo. But first he cuts a piece of red wool from a ball in the sewing basket, pokes it through the hole and hangs the portrait around his neck, under his vest. The wood gets warmer and warmer, the picture sticks to his skin and feels like a brother.

—

When they get home, Mother and the girls are whispering. They look worried, they're talking about Mr Java. They've been to see a specialist, for advice, because Mr Java refuses to see any more doctors and he's stopped taking his tablets – he's had enough. They make him too sleepy, the head of a family has to be alert, especially these days. It will all come good, he says. 'Even without tablets he rots in bed all day,' the girls complain.

The doctor has recommended hearty food: beef tea every day, lots of iron and walnuts, brain food. And fresh vegetables to make him more active. Mother has stocked up with a bag of health and immediately withdraws to the kitchen. When the girls stay away, the boy slips in and creeps up to her, close to her ear, 'May I crack the nuts?'

Mother is washing the sand out of the spinach. 'You made me jump.'

'I'd like to help,' he says in his sweetest voice.

'Please don't, it's already such a mess.'

'I'll crack them over an old newspaper.'

'You're blocking the light.'

'I'll be careful and break them into two halves.'

'So you can pinch the other half, I suppose.'

It's always that way. 'I know a secret,' he says to bring her round.

'Go and bore the girls.'

'I don't want them to know.'

'What is it?'

'Nothing.'

She wraps a wet arm around the boy. 'Come on, you can trust me.' (It's working, it's working!) She dries her hands off on a tea towel, taking the opportunity to clean behind his ears at the same time. He's not used to so much tenderness.

'It's too secret.'

She sits down on the kitchen chair and taps her knee. He crawls on to her lap and pulls the red thread up a little from under his vest . . .

'Stop acting so weird!' (She hasn't noticed . . . She never notices anything.) Mother pushes him off her lap.

—

Mr Java stays in bed but is still there at the table: he's in the scratches in the oilcloth, the stains on the wallpaper, the marks under his chair – all silent evidence of his rage. Mother and the girls serve the spinach-and-nut pancake gloomily, the boy plays with the red thread around his neck ... but they have no time for his fantasies. They're getting a plate ready for Mr Java. He doesn't want anything to eat, he screams from behind the bedroom door, he's scared that Mother will crush a tablet into it first. He only wants a glass of clear water. When no one reacts, he starts screaming, 'Water! Water!'

'He has to get it himself,' says first sister.

'We mustn't give in to him,' says Mother, 'we can't let him become bedridden.'

And all together, 'The doctor said we had to be strict.'

When the boy threatens to get up to take him some water anyway, two rough, sisterly hands push him back down onto his chair. Broth splashes over the table. A piece of spinach-and-nut pancake slides off a plate. A fork jabs into an arm.

'Brat.'

'Bitch.'

A row.

Whether they talk or keep quiet, for the last few weeks they've always ended up fighting at the table. They can't manage to eat peacefully any more, Mr Java's absence doesn't help. Before dinner's cooked, the boy and the girls can play recorder beautifully together and washing up they sing perfect harmonies, but at the table they lash out. They try not to, but it's bigger than they are. 'You're confused,' says Mother, 'all of nature is confused.'

—

The boy is brushing his teeth. Mr Java homes in on the noise and shuffles into the bathroom. He leans on the boy's delicate shoulders and they look at each other in the mirror. The boy fills his glass. 'Are you going to bed already?' asks Mr Java, he'd love to go out, into the fresh air: doctor's orders. Would he like to come too? It's not a command, but a cautious question. Mr Java looks so . . . scared. Scared? No, Mr Java is never scared.

Shall they check the horses? The boy pulls trousers and a pullover on over his pyjamas, together they step out into the night . . . to the stable door, no further. Outside it's muggy and clear, the torch stays in his pocket. Mr Java strokes the hair on the back of the boy's neck. That's how soft his hand can be. A few steps further that same hand jerks the boy's head back to force him to look up. Pupil has to point out Ursa Major and the North Star. The lessons of the great outdoors, practical lessons! And while they try to determine the sidereal time (something neither of them has ever done successfully), Mr Java's unpredictable hand scouts out the collar of his pyjama jacket. What does that hand feel? A thread? He hauls

133

up the picture. The quivering torch lights the portrait. 'Where'd you get this?'

'Found it in a drawer.'

'This isn't for children.' Mr Java rips the thread from the picture. A piece goes flying. 'It's coconut shell, very fragile . . .'

'Is it Mother's?'

'Yes,' says Mr Java. 'Enough questions.'

'The little brother?'

'It's you.'

'Did lots and lots of kids die in the war?'

'Why are you asking that?' Mr Java takes the boy by the chin and stares into his face. 'Not a single life is ever lost in the cosmos, everything comes back as atoms and they become a person or a horse or particles in the Milky Way . . . Things that don't make it always get another chance.'

The boy nods earnestly, trying to understand, and asks himself, Am I that other chance?

The stable key doesn't want to go in the lock, the boy has to provide light. As the door swings open, Mr Java pulls him in with him, breaking their agreement – his arm around his head. The boy tries to wriggle out of his hold but stumbles and is dragged into the stench by the neck, towards the steaming horse dung. 'You have to beat it,' Mr Java says, 'do your best.' The boy refuses to listen, he shakes off the words, kicks free and runs outside . . . A shocked Mr Java watches him go: soon the boy will be telling him what to do.

Buckets scrape over stone, corn rages out of a tin. The boy waits outside panting, washing his lungs with sea air . . . The lantern in the stable has been lit, inside Mr Java talks to the horses . . . His voice is so soft and through the chinks the boy catches glimpses of gestures that are so loving: he rubs the horses, and the horses long for his hand now they've had to go so long without being ridden. The boy sees it through a haze of tears: hard hands rubbing the stiffness out of life-saving horses.

He thinks, If only I'd been born a horse. Being a son is his misfortune, he would have got further as a horse.

the mirror house

Still warm from his hiding place under the mattress, the pilot says, 'Why don't you spend tonight with me in the mirror house?' Since the boy was forced to give up his jacket to clothe the inundated, he has sought the pilot's voice in his exercise book. There he finds support and counsel. When danger threatens, they take cover together in the mirror house.

The mirror house is guaranteed bomb-free. In the mirror house nothing ever goes wrong. Anything that breaks falls back together again of its own accord. The paint glistens like a brand-new pencil. Blows change to caresses, lashes to kisses. Even when there's no sign of trouble, he likes to stroll through the rooms before going to sleep. To check supplies. Inside the mirror house there is enough soap and peanut butter for years. There are never any bikes in the hall, no pedal scratches, no kerosene fumes. The cupboards are neat and tidy. The boy knows the way blind. Even in the daytime he likes to spend time there with the pilot. They get on fine. Sometimes he wishes he could invite the girls. 'Look,' he'd tell them, 'this is our house and this is my secret brother.'

In the ordinary house no one knows about his mirror life, they only see him on the outside: a boy sitting at the table and lying alone in his bed at night. They have no idea how often there are two of him.

the healer

His nose keeps sneezing. Wool and chalk, but the fluff outside as well . . . it's too much for the boy, sometimes he sneezes for thirty minutes on the trot. 'Since the atomic tests it's only got worse,' says Mother.

'Then half the world should be sneezing,' Mr Java says.

'They'll be here to pick him up in a minute . . . let's hope to God it helps.'

It's Sunday, two in the afternoon and the boy is waiting in the hall. A runny nose – that's all that's left of him.

'He's got to beat it himself.' Mr Java is barefoot in his dressing gown and still hasn't shaved.

'It's in the air.' Mother bends down over a suitcase with winter clothes. 'And now it's in him.'

'And Our Father in Heaven has to get it out of him. God is not a hanky.'

'This one's got the gift.'

'The gift of the gab.'

'They say it helps even if you don't believe.'

'Hear that?' Mr Java nudges his son. 'Don't believe in it! Believe in yourself.'

'Get dressed,' Mother tells Mr Java, 'I don't want anyone seeing you like this.'

'I'm not going, am I?'

Mother holds up a duffle coat. 'Put it on,' she snaps at the nose.

'That's how you breed weaklings,' Mr Java sighs, shuffling off to his bedroom.

'They're sending someone on a motorbike with a sidecar,' Mother says apologetically.

The duffle coat smells of mothballs. Sneeze. The boy's eyes start watering . . . the flowers on Mother's blue dress bob round in a big pond. She shakes out the coat and puts a white cotton flying hat on his head. His head jiggles to and fro as she tugs on the strap, the buckle is rusty and pinches the skin under his chin. 'Take it off when you're in front of the healer, otherwise the energy won't get through.'

A dull voice sounds from the bedroom: 'Where are my ankle boots?'

'Get him to look at your father while he's at it,' she whispers into his strapped-down ear, 'he spent the whole morning lying in the dark again.' She slips a photo into the pocket of his coat – Mr Java in uniform, she doesn't have any others – with ten guilders paper-clipped to the back. 'The healer blesses photos too.'

The bell shrills down the hall. 'That'll be them,' calls Mother. Heavy feet scrape on the iron grille in front of the door. A broad shadow moves behind the lace curtain. Mother opens the door: a man in a blue greatcoat steps in, helmet in hand, wearing army boots. A husky voice introduces itself as Worm, Pickle Worm. Mother hesitates before telling him her own first name. 'You *are* picking people up for the healer?'

'And a mighty honour it is, sister, a rare opportunity. This man is an infrequent visitor to these parts.'

Mother looks into his craggy face with surprise, takes a step back and calls him Mr Worm.

'Brother,' he corrects her, 'or just call me Pickle.' Surely she knows him? Or is she new to the village? Everyone knows Pickle . . . Pickle the beachcomber. Hasn't she ever passed his house? Built completedly of driftwood. In his free time he does odd jobs for the brothers and sisters. He subjects the surroundings to a quick appraisal and nods at a crooked door. 'I'd fix that in a jiffy.'

'First the boy,' says Mother.

'May I make your acquaintance as well?' Mr Java asks with a grin, sticking his face around the corner of

140

the bedroom door. But when he sees the helmet and greatcoat, his face darkens and his right hand is startled into a small salute.

'I serve the Lord,' says Pickle.

'In army boots?'

'Never had no blisters,' laughs Pickle, exposing a row of brown teeth.

Mr Java assesses the visitor silently. Pickle rocks from one boot to the other. Mr Java straightens his dressing gown, and stalks up to the beachcomber. 'And what's this miraculous cure going to put us back?' he asks with outstretched hand.

'Ah, we're all Christians . . .'

'Exactly.'

'The Lord will reward us . . .'

'In the meantime,' says Mr Java, 'I'm sure you'd like a cup of tea or coffee? It will only take a minute. I'd like to find out what we can expect. Get to know you a little.'

Pickle is in a hurry, the other boys are waiting outside, the healer is a busy man, he's travelling on in the evening.

The boy looks at the dented helmet. 'Is that a Kraut helmet?'

'I wear what the sea gives me. I never buy nothing in shops.' His coat is RAF, trousers and jacket are from a Canadian who washed up on shore – 'They still had his name on the inside. I even have a pair of pilot's sunglasses from China, kept afloat by the Lord all the way to our beach.'

'The Lord's already rewarded you then,' says Mr Java. 'Christian, very Christian . . . ransacking dead soldiers.' His lips form angry words, but they stay silent, he swallows them and turns around furiously. The bedroom door slams shut, so hard the knob shakes. The door opens again. Mr Java's head stabs through the opening. 'Turn it down, let the boy stay home, turn it down. . .' He shuts the door. Bedsprings squeak, wood splinters. They hear a muffled, 'Sorry, sorry.' Mother and the boy look down at the floor silently. They see what they hear: Mr Java throwing himself on the bed, his fists battering the panel.

'Did I . . . has the bro . . . is something wrong?' Pickle looks anxiously at Mother.

'Where I'm going,' asks the boy, 'what's it called?'

Pickle bends over confidentially. 'The man you will soon see was born with a caul,' he whispers.

'We're so glad you can take him,' says Mother.

'It might benefact your husband as well.'

'There's nothing wrong with me!' Mr Java shouts from behind the door.

Mother wraps a scarf around her son's neck.

'Not so tight, you're choking me . . .'

'If it gets late, keep him warm.'

'We won't be there on our lonesome,' says Pickle, 'plenty of folk are coming to the polder.' He takes the boy by the hand, Mother follows them down the garden path. Behind their backs, a fist pounds the bedroom window, a ring raps the glass. Mother lays her hand on the flying hat. 'Don't look back.'

The window slides up. 'Believe in yourself, turn it down.'

'Open your heart and mind,' Mother says, before running back to the house.

'Can I wear the helmet?' asks the boy.

—

A motorbike with sidecar is gleaming on the pavement. An old, silver Harley-Davidson, but the sidecar is a converted bathtub with two short-back-and-sides sticking up out of it. Pickle slaps the back of a wedge-shaped head, 'This is Henkie.' Henkie nods in agreement. The other one is called Rick and has an open harelip; his fingers are covered with silver paint. 'In

143

all the constiration, I've forgot your name.' All three of them look at him expectantly.

The nose sniffs, swallows. Behind him a window slides down, curtains whizz shut.

'Soon you'll have to say your name loud and clear, otherwise the Lord won't be able to help you.'

The nose investigates the motorbike. The petrol tank, the weather-beaten canvas stretched over the sidecar tub, the sunburnt necks of the boys, they stink . . . everything stinks, of paint – wet, reeking silver paint. Pipes, mudguards, rims, spokes, handlebars – they haven't missed a single weld.

'What are you waiting for? Get in. Mr Raumuller can't hang around for ever.' Pickle bangs the tub with his hand. Mr Raumuller can make blood clot, his hand can seal wounds and raise invalids up on to their own two feet. After a prayer meeting they personally push their wheelchairs into the ditch. There *is* no greater healer. 'If we're too late, he won't be able to present you to the Lord,' says Pickle. The sidecar shudders impatiently.

Pickle lifts the boy up, the buttons of his greatcoat sliding past the toggles of the duffle coat, then plonks him down between the legs of wedge-headed Henkie and harelipped Rick's back. When the motorbike takes off, Rick's drool goes flying past his hat. The boy recoils. Henkie thumps the intruder in the back. Buttocks

144

squeeze between thighs, shoes scrape over calves, elbows jab and the sidecar rocks like a barge at sea. Pickle warns the three of them to sit still, his hand lashes out over their heads, the wheel of the sidecar goes off the road, grass swishes past the mudguard. Pickle clenches his knuckles white trying to straighten the swerving motorbike. He curses under his breath . . . 'Forgimme those words, forgimme those words.'

Thrips dance over the road, it's warmer away from the coast, they spatter all over the motorbike. The white flying hat is covered with stains. The sidecar is sticky. There is a hole on one side of the tub; above it, letters bulge through the silver paint: an E . . . a B . . . EBEN HAEZER & CO. NEW YORK. The nose sniffs up the letters, traces them with its fingers, spells them out in its head . . . It doesn't understand the strange symbol. It writes the name blind with one nail on its thigh . . . It feels them again, practising softly. The paint comes off.

The road along the canal is busy. On the right are signs with arrows pointing up at an angle. Raumuller. They say Raumuller in fat red letters. After each sign the wind buffets their ears. Pickle points at the name and gives the thumbs-up. Cars look for parking spaces on the side of the dike, a bus is stuck in the mud. Pickle swerves around it skilfully. Raumuller. Raumuller . . . *rau rau*, sing the spokes.

The motorbike slows down. Snatches of music wash over the dike. The boys clamber over each other to look around . . . there . . . yes, two flags are fluttering down below. The motorbike leaves the asphalt to jolt down a tractor path to a lower field. The side mirrors of parked cars catch the sun, everywhere there are people in hats, black hats. Behind an orchard, next to a ditch, there is something white and shining. 'Circus,' lisps Rick.

'The healing tent,' Pickle corrects him.

The afternoon sun colours the canal a deep navy and the dark water stains the grass blue, along with the trousers of the salvationists, the nurses' aprons, the caps and hats with bows, the embroidery on the collars, the trim and the bands with *JESUS SAVES. RAUMULLER. RAUMULLER. PRAISE THE LORD ALL HIS HOSTS.* The boy spells out the blue words in silence, feels for hair peeking out from under his flying hat and pushes back a curl.

The sidecar tears past wheelchairs and giant tricycles. A forest of crutches, braces and walking sticks blocks their path. Stumbling neckless hunchbacks, hydrocephalics, cripples with their shoes on the wrong feet. The grass has been jabbed to sludge; beside them a man is carrying a pale girl in his arms, the blanket hanging straight down from her knees.

Pickle is not having any dilly-dallying. He parks, tosses his helmet into the sidecar and herds the trio into the tent. Past the row of cripples, past the imbeciles swaying in time to the music coming over the PA system. Henkie grunts and wobbles, Pickle pushes him on. At the entrance there are stencils with songs and verses from the Bible. The boys grab at the pile but a loud voice stops them. 'Who sees us? Who knows us? Who heals us?'

The voice is coming from the healing tent. A muggy warmth wafts out to meet them. The boy has to sneeze; he blows his nose on his scarf, stuffs it in the pocket of his coat and keeps the flying hat on his head. He thinks, Rick spits blood, Henkie looks like a moron . . . but a tickle in your nose, can the healer see a tickle? Walking past the trestle table at the entrance, he drags his right leg.

A woman behind a pile of cards gives them a friendly smile. 'What do you have, brother?'

'Three, sister.' Pickle pulls the boys up close.

The sister takes three cards with dangling cords from a pile. 'Names?' She can hardly make herself heard. At the front, near the stage, people are already singing along. Two salvationists carry in a table, they fold out a light-blue cloth and pin posters with Raumuller's photo to the edges – piercing eyes, brushy hair . . . no caul. Rick and Henkie are abbreviations, the sister doesn't write them down. She wants their full names. Rick expands himself to Richard – pronouncing the *ch* as *sh*. The sister still isn't satisfied. 'Your baptismal names.'

'Peter . . . Paul,' says Rick.

'Surname?'

'. . . Van Pee.'

'That's the Ps covered,' says Pickle. Dribble falls down on to the card. The sister wipes it off the table with a smile. Henkie becomes Hendrick Jacob Wokke.

'And you?' the sister asks the boy, who wipes his nose on his sleeve.

He hesitates . . . thinking. The sister's ballpoint taps on the table, she plays with the button, her smile grows more strained every second. A ray of sunlight falls through the opening in the tent. The silver cross on her left breast lights up. The cross is panting in time with her chest. The boy feels in his pocket and digs out the photo of Mr Java. It's crumpled, the ten-guilder note is gone from under the paper clip.

'Has he lost his tongue?' asks the sister.

The boy bends over to look on the ground, 'No, my money.'

'You have to say your name, loud and clear, otherwise Mr Raumuller can't present you to the Lord,' says Pickle.

'What's a baptismal name?'

'D'you hear that, sister? D'you hear that, boys? He doesn't even know his baptismal name. The ninnies they give me . . . Come on,' Pickle tugs on his duffle-coat, 'you must have been baptised, to wash away your sins. Come on, what's your Sunday name?'

The boy counts off the days of the week. Friday is a name, for a native, and Sunday is dustday, the day they eat zwieback . . . but he's never heard of any Sunday names at home. Pickle gives the boy a shaking. 'Unless you've got a baptismal name you can't get healed.'

The boy nods his head with every word Pickle says. The Lord can't just perform His miracles nilly-willy. He has to know who He's dealing with, name and address – the whole caboodle, just like the postman. A baptismal name is a blessing, God's stamp of approval. The Children's Bible echoes through his head . . . the picture book Mother reads out loud at Easter and Christmas, so quietly that in the end he can't hear the words. It never mentioned baptism, maybe he didn't pay attention, he doesn't like the Children's Bible, no matter how good Jesus is at magic tricks. If Mother reads out of the Bible for too long, Mr Java clenches his fists until he's squeezed the blood out of his fingers.

'What's wrong with you?' Pickle asks the boy.

'Allergy,' he says anxiously. He shows him the photo of Mr Java.

'What am I supposed to do with that?'

149

'It has to be blessed too.'

The photo is smeared with paint, a silver stripe runs over Mr Java's uniform. The queue behind them pushes forward; the top of the table slides back over the trestles. Pickle grabs the photo out of the boy's hands, looks at Mr Java in uniform and growls at the brat beneath him, 'Does your father go to church?'

The boy shrugs.

'But your family is in the Lord?'

'My father hates the Lord.'

Indignation behind Pickle's back. Rick blows a bubble of drool. Henkie stops grunting.

'That's what I waste my petrol money on,' Pickle sighs, 'serving a bunch of heathens.' He takes the boy by both shoulders and pushes him up against the table. 'Put him down for the tub,' he tells the sister. 'Unless you're baptised you're on a highway to hell.'

The boy sniffs his silver fingers with embarrassment. It's as if all the names in his head have been painted over, not a single letter is showing through, nothing is called what it's supposed to be called . . . He wipes his hands on his trousers, over his thighs. 'Eben,' he wavers, 'my baptismal name is Eben Ra . . . hazer.'

'What?' asks Pickle. 'Eben? That's a Kraut name.'

'My father fought for the Allies.'

'You don't say? And then he thought, why not . . . we'll baptise him Eben . . . Eben.' Pickle looks at him mockingly and taps his helmet. 'Our healer is German, not all Germans are bad. He'll know the name – Eben Razer, Eben Razer . . . Have you ever heard such a weird name, sister? They don't even give ships names like that, and I've seen plenty of names wash up on the beach. Ebb 'n' Raiser. It sounds like a name for the sea.'

The boy helps him spell it. 'Eben Razer,' he says, smoothly this time. He likes it: this new, cast-iron name. Even though he hadn't wanted to lie at all.

'Mr Raumuller will present you to the Lord . . . better saved than sorry. Only those He has received count,' says Pickle solemnly.

The sister asks for a date of birth as well, but Eben Razer is not saying another word. Pickle pulls him towards the stage, another sister takes charge of Rick and Henkie. Eben Razer races past rows of invalids – in bandages or wheelchairs or lying on sloping shuffleboards on wheels, being pushed in or out by salvationists – he grazes his ankle on an iron leg brace and is lifted up on to the stage with a grimace of pain on his face. 'There, in that corner, and wait till they come for you,' Pickle snaps at him.

Eben Razer limps over to the spot.

'Who sees us, who knows us, who heals us?' repeats a salving voice over a PA the brass band drowns out. Trumpet players walk out on to the stage, feet and cheeks moving in time. People push forward. Rick and Henkie are at the front, pointing, staring . . . they nudge each other, they're talking about him, the heathen from the sidecar. Sisters push the last wheelchairs up to the steps that lead to the stage. Two salvationists hurry out with a tub of water. A buzz goes through the crowd.

Eben Razer shuffles back as far as he can, until he feels a post against his shoulder. He looks up, away from the people below him, looking for the all-seeing eye. His gaze follows the ropes, the joins in the canvas – the strap of the flying hat cuts into his throat . . . until he's dizzy and has to grab the post. A lukewarm wind moves over his cheeks . . . it's a hand, a hand floating above his face, a hand in a white dress. Eben Razer ducks out of the way. But two black eyes push him back up against the post, they stare at him, eyes under a brush of black hair. People applaud, the hand pushes his head down . . . the people are clapping him. Eben Razer glows. His whole body tingles . . . The hand makes Eben Razer bow low . . . He bows and grows at the same time. What should he look like? A pilot after a successful mission? A general taking the salute? He looks out over the crowd as if he's a picture in a newspaper. He's already cutting himself out.

Numbed, he lets two salvationists lead him to the blue-covered table. The tent has stopped clapping, people push forward, uproar. The man in the white dress raises a hand . . . the tent falls silent. Eben Razer trembles . . . So this is Raumuller: the healer in person.

Raumuller leads them in prayer. He thanks the Lord for letting him preach in a Dutch polder. Eben Razer stares at the hem of the talking dress. The hem swings over the planks, the hem walks to the steps . . . Invalids and their helpers surge around him. Names crackle over the PA, the baptismal names of the sick. Raumuller touches them on the forehead, some of them fall asleep immediately, others start to cry, and one – *yes, look, look*, the tent rejoices – one woman grabs hold of her helper, she tries to stand up out of her wheelchair, her feet hesitate, she wobbles . . . she . . . yes, she takes her helper's hand and walks. The jubilation washes out against the canvas. 'Seeing is be-lieeeeeving,' Raumuller peals into the microphone. 'Yesssss,' those present cry, 'yes, it's the truth . . . aaaaamen.' He wraps an arm around the woman's shoulders and praises Jesus who walked on the water, and the invalids who are now standing in the polder, on land that was once sea. 'Isn't that *wunderbar*!'

'Yesssss!'

In Paradise there were no seas. Seas arose after the Flood . . . 'The Flood, the Flood,' echoes through the rows. The Hollanders reclaimed land from the sea.

153

Thus the Lord gave them dry land under their feet again. Faith is like a polder and God is a windmill, pumping out the water. From the wet to the dry. Hallelujah!

Eben Razer is pushed towards the tub, Mr Java's photo clamped to his chest. He holds up the photo . . . but Mr Raumuller is talking with his eyes shut, blessing, baptising with his eyes shut . . . and Eben Razer lets it all happen: again that warm hand, on his forehead this time, a drum roll. He goes up and down, in and out of the water. He swallows, the edge of the tub cuts into his throat . . . small and dripping, he hears for the first time in his life that he is not made of flesh and bones and water, ninety-five per cent water as Mr Java has taught him, but of dust – the dust he's so allergic to!

The salvationists let go: Eben Razer runs off the stage. He's not limping any more, he even swallows a sneeze as Pickle rubs him dry in the panels of his RAF greatcoat. Back through the polder, in the bathtub on wheels, holding Mr Java's photo up in the wind. From the wet to the dry.

———

'Once but never again,' Pickle tells Mother as he delivers Eben to the door. What a ninny she gave him, turned away from the Lord, lost and living in sin, child of retrobates . . . and the Lord this and the Lord that . . . but fortunately he's now saved, *he* at least is saved . . . thanks to the healer and thanks to Pickle, a beachcomber who can build temples out of flotsam and jetsam. Praise the Lord!

The boy shivers in his duffle coat.

'Ah, he's always got something,' says Mother.

Mr Java emerges from the bedroom, pale and still unshaven. 'And?' he asks with a vicious grin.

A wet sneeze resounds in the hall.

Mr Java pulls a white handkerchief out of his dressing-gown pocket . . . starched, ironed with a military crease. 'Egyptian linen,' he says, 'for you.'

Pickle shakes his head and swings on his heel. Mother frees her son from the flying hat. 'Didn't you feel anything at all?' She rubs away the red stripes on his cheeks, squeezes blood out of the wound under his chin. 'You did hand in the photo?'

'Yes,' the boy croaks, 'I have been received.'

—

The boy is lying on his bed, the handkerchief spread out over his face. He breathes in the smell of laundry, looks up through the linen, exploring the shapes of the room blindfolded. He imagines that he is a patient wrapped in bandages, a soldier in a field hospital. Unshaven, pale . . . Nurses walk by, stop and call for help. Outside someone plays the trumpet. Mr Java's photo is resting in his hands . . . soldier, he never made it any higher, but now a beautiful silver stripe adorns his uniform. Today he will receive an even higher promotion, to the heavens. He will present him to the Lord. The bath is waiting. Two taps on, hot and cold at once. While filling it, he prays and begs that Mr Java will rise up out of darkness and stop hurling plates of food at the wallpaper. If you're not baptised you're on a highway to hell. He launches the photo. Mr Java floats . . . looking up to heaven and spinning around above the plughole, where the water gurgles away quietly . . . the photo curls . . . and sinks. The boy lays the portrait on the handkerchief to dry; a black trickle soaks into the linen. The uniform has washed off. Leaving the silver medal.

the report

Mr Java has arisen out of darkness. He has slept the last poison from the tablets out of his system and is feeling much better. Totally relaxed, a question of headpower – he says. The fists in his pockets tell a different story: his trouser seams are about to burst.

It's report time.

The girls already have theirs, their schoolbags are lying idle in a corner and Mother has looked over their marks approvingly. Mr Java doesn't get to see a thing, he doesn't ask either, *they* have to come to him. He is waiting impatiently for another report: his pupil's radiant results. In the end the girls show their wisdom (at Mother's insistence) by lining up before him as if butter wouldn't melt in their mouths, report books in hand – and hair on end the moment he starts harping about Cs that should have been Bs, and Bs that could have been better. The best isn't good enough for Mr Java. After shaking off a pat on the shoulder, middle sister snaps at Mother, 'He has no right . . . We're better educated now than he ever was.'

Yes, report time is a time to relax.

'And where's yours?' asks Mother.

'It's coming,' says the boy.

Mr Java doesn't ask anything. He waits and clenches his fists . . .

'We should have had it long ago,' says Mother.

No, Mother doesn't need to make any phone calls. The headmaster still has to sign it. The teacher was ill.

'I hope your report is better than your excuse.'

The boy has been looking pale these last few days. He needs more time to think up a good reason for failing. This will be the first report Mr Java sees, he tore up the last one and told lie after lie to family and school: no results yet because he started late in the year, Mother gone away to her flooded family, Mr Java seriously ill, report stolen . . . His teacher has been trying to speak to his parents for months, giving him letters he didn't pass on and posting others he managed to intercept at home. This close to the summer holidays there's no wriggling out of it, they want to see a report and they won't take no for an answer. Unless something terrible happens . . . An accident? If you're sick people forgive you anything. Should he take a razor blade to his forehead, wrap himself in a bloody bandage or almost choke on an allergy? He's used all those acts before, this time he has to come up with something better.

It hasn't gone well at school. Mr Java's promising pupil is behind instead of ahead. His handwriting was rejected on the very first day. 'Sloping? Who taught you that?' asked the teacher. 'In this country we write straight up and down.' He never dared to tell Mr Java, for him he kept writing sloping. Lots of the things he learnt at home – supported by pictures and tracing – were greeted with howls of derision in the class. Sidereal time? Overseas territories, rubber-tapping, tobacco cultivation, pepper gardens? They only shrugged. Winning medals, miraculous fakirs, the stability of proas, pensions and clipping vouchers, the radio news, the grave situation in Korea, the Iron Curtain, A-bomb, H-bomb, his lists of difficult words (including a few English ones!) – these children didn't know a thing: even 'inundated' meant nothing to them. 'Stop showing off!' And that expensive pencil could go straight back in his bag. Pen and penwiper were the rule here. 'You're not a carpenter, are you?' He had to start at the very beginning, all over again, with sums too (even though he was good at them). Since then he's written back-to-front more and more often, and turned all the numbers round as well. School exercise book and home exercise book, pencil and pen . . . they have become separate worlds and he does his best to keep them apart.

How can he explain failing to Mr Java? Behind his back, he's brave enough. Planning things with the mirror pilot, he knows no fear. Why does he shrivel up as soon as he's in front of him? If only he had a fraction of the girls' cheek. They can be so hard and strong. The thought alone makes the boy feel even more helpless.

Maybe he should write him a letter. Like the ones Mr Java writes himself, a letter that will put everything right again. He can already hear it resounding in his head, masterful sentences. An honest letter with a straight margin. He'll show what he's made of. He'll promise to improve. He sharpens the last new Koh-I-Noor. His weapon in distress.

—

The next day after school, with Mr Java at the stable and Mother washing corn salad in the kitchen, the boy lays his report next to the sink. Casually, with his pencil behind his ear. The report has spent half a week under his mattress, next to the exercise book with the mirror pilot. The bedsprings have left their mark. Big fat zeros.

'Finally,' says Mother. 'Congratulations.'

Ashamed, the boy doesn't say a word.

She quickly dries her hands on her apron and opens the report . . . She shakes her head at every subject. A drop falls from the report. 'That's impossible! A U for writing?'

'That's U for unsatisfactory.'

'But you're so good at it?'

'I know.' He hands her the letter.

'What am I supposed to do with this?'

'From me, for Mr Java, read it . . .'

Mother unfolds it. 'What a scrawl. You call those letters . . . I can't read that.' She hands it back unread. And, while fishing bits of corn salad out of the sink with a bitter expression, 'We should have waited before having you. I was too weak, your father was too weak . . . it wasn't a healthy start . . . this is what comes of it.'

———

They have to wait for Mr Java, who stays away longer than usual: he's giving the lifeboat horses extra attention after being ill for so long. The boy keeps a lookout at the window. The report book is warming up in his hands, the letter is in an envelope between its pages. Mr Java looks at him expectantly as he walks up the path . . . but the boy doesn't dare to hold up the report. He hears his shoes in the hall. Will Mother be the first to tell him? She runs to the toilet and rattles the hook.

A weary Mr Java steps into the room and sees what the boy is holding in his hands. 'Ah, let's see how you've done.' He brushes the straw off his trousers,

161

moves the chair closer to the window ... makes himself comfortable ... opens the report ... looks, reads, sighs ... The report falls to his lap. Mr Java turns pale, covers his face with his hands. The letter slips to the floor. The boy picks it up, flaps it in front of Mr Java's eyes, taps him on the hands with it. Wanting to whisper something in his ear, he bends forward but stops with a start ... the smell of the stable keeps him at arm's length ... No, it's not the horses. It's Mr Java flinching back. The pencil behind the boy's ear has stabbed him in the cheek ... 'Shall I read it?' he whispers.

'What?' Mr Java asks numbly.

'The letter.'

'That teacher's mad.'

'Here.' The boy lays the letter on his lap.

Mr Java opens it and reads: ... Dear Sir ... I hereby promise ... 'Your handwriting used to be like mine,' says Mr Java dully.

Betrayal. The boy has written straight by accident. Slowly the pupil is outgrowing his teacher.

the newspaper photo

There is a boy at the front of the line, a Chink with an empty bowl in each hand, wearing a short blue coat. Behind the boy there are hundreds more, all in the same coats, all gazing expectantly at pans of steaming rice. They are communist POWs, drafted young and overrun by war . . . Their faces are dusty. Half-way down the line there is a boy with a striped mattress on his back, head to the ground, bent under his burden. The sky is greyer than the ground. COMMUNISTS FLEE, says the newspaper.

'Never take your mattress,' says Mr Java. 'Travel light, yes. You have to travel light. A blanket's better.'

summer

A long summer has begun. A summer in which the family does its best to forget. Golden old days when everything is the way it must have been and should have stayed – warm, very warm and lazy – without news from conference tables, without the dark voices of news-readers. The hostile camps needed a break . . . the guns fell silent. Mother catches Mr Java whistling at the window. He's embarrassed by his own cheerfulness, but she takes it as a sign. 'To the beach, get the bedspread out of the wardrobe!'

The bedspread is a family institution. It is a tabernacle of purity, a giggling refuge from impropriety. The girls start by unfolding it in the hall to make a big knapsack. The suntan lotion goes in, books, sandtrap sandwiches, the ball. Cardigans for in the wind. Shovel, bucket, the old bus tyre inner tube. They tie the corners together and balance the bedspread on the deckchair Mother will catch her fingers in later. Mr Java and the boy are the bearers. They take everything upon themselves.

The family goes to the beach dressed, sunny but decent, not like city people who step out of the train in bathing suits. Or Germans, in bathrobes. It's in the heat that you display self-control: Mr Java in a tie and Mother in a hat. True colonial manners.

It is only on the beach – the quiet one – that the great change begins. Mother goes behind the bedspread first, Mr Java stands on his toes and holds the corners up high with both hands, head turned to study invisible ships. The girls are already sitting and blowing the sand out of their books. The boy turns his lotioned back to the changing session and starts digging. Every now and then, still digging, he looks back with his head between his legs: thank goodness, no nudity in sight. Then the girls go behind the bedspread and Mother takes over from Mr Java. Both his arms have gone to sleep. He doesn't get changed himself, strangers aren't allowed to see his scars – 'They'd think I was a Kraut.'

Mother watches her daughters enviously – slim and a beautiful brown. They hand her their clothes . . . a bra falls on to the sand. Mother bends down, the bedspread bends with her. The boy points at a bit of bare breast. He whoops. Girlish screams. And then, as if someone else has crept into his mouth, he purses his lips and whistles – high, low and loud, like a street urchin. Mr Java rushes up to him and boxes his ears. His hand isn't even drowsy.

165

The girls slide their thumbs under the shoulder straps of their swimming costumes, straighten the smocking at the front and walk towards him. Bedspread stretched between them. He turns into a bull: thrusting forward. But they seize him, pinion his arms behind his back and press him down on the bedspread. They grab a corner each and toss him in the air – he almost slides out. Mother rushes to help: four pairs of hands pull the bedspread tight, turning it into a trampoline, a rag doll bounces up and down, up and down, high and deep. He lies on his back and floats. He bumps into their bellies and breasts – a wall of flesh, impassable. They throw him higher. He rolls towards them. From one to the other. Choking with laughter.

'He's braying, he's braying,' the girls call in turn.

mumbling

Mr Java comes back from the hotel with his hands black from all those papers. His face looks just as black . . . Without greeting anyone, he walks straight to his place at the window. The boy is doing his homework at the table and hears him mumble, 'Aspirin, safety pins, sandbags, methylated spirits, burner, toilet paper, candles, rubber gloves, flea powder, Listerine, bandages, iodine, hardtack, soap, white clothes . . . stripes and flowers burn patterns on your skin. Remember: tell Mother and the girls that people with white clothes were burnt less in Hiroshima . . . White, safe tropical white.'

The boy looks quizzically at the black shadow.

'The Russians have got it now too,' says Mr Java. 'We're ready for it, bring on the hydrogen bomb.'

The carefree summer is over.

foreign

The storms mould the dunes and the horizon behind the house blows away on the wind. After a strong northwester, flat tops are suddenly crests and familiar peaks are rounded off. The marram grass has lost its grip. Sand swirls through the streets, the squares are covered. It even finds its way inside. Grains of sand crunch in the hall and scratch in bed. When the girls brush their hair in the morning, it hails in the sink. Shutters bang day and night. The stove can't cope and an icy wind blows up out of the unflushable toilet. Nature really is confused.

There are flowers on the windows in the bedroom. The boy has five blankets piled on his bed. He has just woken from his own voice and although he doesn't know what he said, he is sure that he must have been talking about his secret in his sleep. He hopes no one else heard it. Are they awake yet? He can't hear anything from the girls' bedroom.

Later, after school, he'll see if his secret is still there. Maybe it's pulled loose, or sailed off under its own steam . . . With this weather nothing stays the same.

This afternoon he will climb up on to the beached ship again . . . and then something will happen. He feels it. He has to share his secret with someone. It's too much for him alone.

A winter storm has tossed a Liberty ship up on to the beach, the whole country knows that – no lifeboats involved, it just suddenly appeared one morning a month ago, at the foot of the dune in front of the hotel, close to the marine aquarium. A rusty tub with a Greek crew, sailing under the Panamanian flag: the *Katingo*. One tug company after another has tried to refloat it, sending out ridiculous little boats with arm-thick hawsers, but it hasn't budged. New storms have only pushed it further up the beach. After that a suction dredger was towed in to make a deep channel. It didn't help . . .

Meanwhile the shopkeepers have been thanking their lucky stars. The newspapers keep writing about the village and day-trippers come and go. The herring man hauled his cart out from its winter sleep and started selling pea soup – on the second day, before anybody else had thought of it. A chippie from Amsterdam set up a stall. The boulevard has never smelt so good. Seagulls warm up in the fumes. None of the family had ever seen chips in a bag before. In the very first week, the shops started selling postcards of the *Katingo* on the beach. The hotel is doing a brisk summer's trade. The whole village is in turmoil.

The boy too. Since the beaching he's gone to check the progress every day, straight from school, bent into the icy storm, hand in hand with Mr Java, because there's a lot to learn. The cane is back in service as a piece of chalk and the beach is a blackboard . . . Mr Java explains the workings of a suction dredger to anyone who wants to know. Yes, he has seen quite a bit of maritime engineering at close hand. In his day in the tropics they never stopped dredging and he knows the sea's whims from experience. You have to watch out for this and for that, and you always have to dig wider, not deeper . . . and, above all, you have to know the currents. But how well do these dredger crews know *our* rips and eddies? *Our*: the day-trippers didn't notice the pride he put into that word, but the boy did . . . Mr Java was doing his best to belong.

Not everyone shared in the happiness and pride. For weeks now the *Katingo*'s crew have been looking on with nothing to do. The Greeks have all been fired. No prospects and not a penny's pay. The council has put them up in the Sea House for the time being and small dark men with black hair and woolly hats now walk through the village at night, with all doors shut against their peering eyes.

Mr Java wanted to ask them in. A Liberty ship, he wanted to know more about that, they'd supplied Europe during the war. And under the Panamanian flag! Freebooters who didn't recognise borders.

Serving the highest bidder. There were no Iron Curtains at sea: Russia, Korea – the *Katingo* had been there, they knew the escape routes, the safe havens, the immigrant countries, the movements of the war fleets . . . They had seen Hiroshima with their own eyes. That was important for the boy as well: geography was strolling past their front door. Foreigners could teach you things. 'And wouldn't you like the smell of a ship in the house again?' he asked to win Mother over. Yes, they had good memories of being at sea, but the way Java piled it on! She had seen him outside accosting the seamen, gesticulating wildly, because all they spoke was Greek, and hadn't their reactions been anything but outgoing? A cup of tea in the house was not going to loosen their tongues and what did they know about politics anyway . . . One look at the poor wretches told you enough.

Still, she too had peered at the gloomy troop from behind the kitchen curtain and pulled a tin of apricots out of the cupboard to dreamily rub the label. 'Greeks love apricots,' she said. But the girls didn't want any bother. There had been enough trouble in the house since Mr Java stopped taking his medicine. Do not disturb! They were getting ready for exam week.

'This is your chance to practise your Greek,' said Mr Java.

First sister laughed in his face, 'They speak Modern Greek.' Anyway, she could only read the letters, that was all the nuns in the camp had taught her. No, the girls thought they were spooky.

The boy isn't worried about the fate of the crew, he can only think of his secret. Soon he'll climb up on to the Liberty ship, using the tall wooden staircase the village carpenter built for the pilots. He is one of six boys the postman has authorised to deliver a Greek newspaper, sent daily by the embassy. All the boys in the village drew straws for it: he got Wednesday, as the youngest. This will be the third time he's allowed on the ship. All by himself, sixty feet up, if not more, at a steep angle, with trembling knees. The first time it was more that he had to, because there was no question of turning back half-way: Mr Java's eyes were burning at the bottom of the stairs and beat him up step by step. The second time he was already less scared and very keen, his curiosity gave him strength, because inside the ship he had discovered something very special: a strange woman, brown from the equator. You didn't need to go overseas to make discoveries. He had spotted her slipping into a cabin, on a cold rusty corridor, when he was wandering around with the newspaper. None of the other newspaper boys knew about her, he had ferreted that out of them. Nobody had ever seen her in the village. Was she a freebooter? Or had she hidden in a cabin as a stowaway? Besides the captain, a few engineers and two pilots, everyone had been ordered off the ship. A refugee, maybe? But one with diamond earrings –

and those eyes, so black, with even more black around them . . . Those eyes will help him up the stairs.

—

Soon after the one o'clock news – just back from school – the boy hurries to the ship. Mr Java has already picked the newspaper up from the post office and walks along beside him, of course he does, but this time he has another goal: he wants to go on board with him.

'You can't,' the boy says.

Mr Java wants to speak to the captain.

'No!' the boy says insistently – too insistently; he tempers his insolent tone, 'Er . . . really, you can't, no one's allowed to disturb him, only the pilot.'

'And you?'

'I just lay the newspaper in front of his door.'

'Why'd you stay away so long last time then?'

'They let me watch.'

Mr Java sends out another line . . . maybe he can give him his card, just go part of the way up the stairs?

'It's not for old men,' says the boy.

Mr Java straightens his back and holds out his cane. 'Here. Carry this.'

—

'Hurry up,' snarls a man from the dredger as the boy comes walking up the beach with Mr Java. He looks at his watch and up at the ship. What's the hurry, does he suspect something? 'The paper was late,' the boy says coolly. Trembling he climbs up next to the rusty hull. Mr Java doesn't watch: he snatched his cane back with annoyance and is ready for lessons in the sand.

Up at the railing a uniformed pilot is waiting. He too looks at his watch. Are they keeping their eyes on him? The boy holds the newspaper up for all to see, the newspaper is his pass. He knows the way to the cabin and slips off between hawsers and crates. The corridor smells of oil and hums and shakes underfoot. The engineers are testing the engines.

When the boy is standing in front of her cabin and mustering his courage, the woman opens the door before he's had a chance to knock. She was lying in wait and pulls him in. Even before he's got his coat off, he's already biting into a dripping honey cake. She wipes a trickle of honey off his chin and smiles at him. She's dressed more beautifully than the other times – in a skimpy black dress, short and unwintry – and is even browner than he thought, almost as brown as the girls, but the things she makes him feel, he never felt with them. She speaks Greek, he knows that because she's reading out loud from the paper. She speaks English as well and doesn't mind the boy not understanding. His mouth has to eat, drink – bottles of lemonade pop open. *How do you do . . .*

sorry, yes and *no*, he runs through his whole supply of English for her . . . but the answers are over his head. He understands her gestures better: a hand inviting him to come and sit next to her on the bed, an elbow moving up to let him in behind the opened newspaper, between her warm, bare arms – with his coat still on. She spells out the Greek letters for him, they're all back to front. The boy doesn't know what to be most surprised about, but one thing is sure: there's no war raging in the Greek newspaper. She reads so calmly, this foreigner, without shaking hands, without rage. There aren't any planes or soldiers in the splotchy photos. *No bomb?* She smiles inside her newspaper . . . he slides even closer to her. '*Yes*,' he sighs and sniffs up the printer's ink without sneezing.

His happiness is disturbed: footsteps clatter down the corridor, the cabin door swings open without knocking, cold rushes in against the newspaper. A belly steps in, a belly with gold buttons: the captain himself. With his brow puckered under the peak of his cap. For a moment the boy thinks that he has now found the woman. Did they follow him, did he betray her? But the captain and the woman know each other, they talk in their fast language, the captain points to the corridor, and at him, '*Naughty boy*.' No, he's not angry. The captain pinches the boy's cheek. '*How do you do?*' Outside, says the captain's thumb, on deck. The woman wraps a shawl around her shoulders and trips along behind him, in high heels.

175

There are voices on deck, coming from above below behind, the engineers are in an uproar. The pilot is bending down over the railing. The boy hears a man shouting, an agitated but familiar sound. It's Mr Java. He's half-way up the stairs and waving his cane around. 'No,' shouts the pilot. '*Back, back,*' shouts the captain. I'm coming, waves the boy. The woman laughs at Mr Java's frantic gestures. '*Father?*' The boy looks at a patch of rust at his feet. No, that's not his father. He takes a step back, away from the pilot's mocking, Yesssss, it is, it's his father all right. Listen to him, the idiot, the fool . . . Are the people on the beach laughing at him? Wait, he'll come straight down. No, you don't, the pilot stops the boy. The wooden stairs are swaying, Mr Java has to calm down first. But Mr Java isn't listening, he doesn't go back down. Mr Java comes on up.

A cane is held out and Mr Java climbs on board puffing and panting. Hat off, hat on. A bow, a hand-shake, a kiss on the back of a hand . . . (And giggles as thanks from the freezing woman.) The visiting card. And a flood of English words, '*Yes, yes, Liberty ship . . . The girls.*'

'*Girls?*' repeats the surprised captain.

The boy doesn't know where to look. The woman and the captain whisper to each other . . . Mr Java doesn't leave them alone, he jokes and clowns around, and laughs when they laugh. He wants something from them . . . '*No? Yes?*' The boy has never seen Mr Java like this before, he is more foreign to him than the foreigners.

'*No. Yes.*' Yes it is.

They fetch thick coats. The captain takes the pilot to one side, there are yells, orders, the stamping falls silent below. Something is about to happen. Mr Java is helped back over the railing, the staircase sways against the side of the ship and he descends – grinning. Only when he is back on the sand does the woman follow. On stilettos! Her dress and coat flutter up. Mr Java holds the staircase still at the bottom without looking up, head turned towards the dunes. The picture of colonial manners.

When the boy and the captain are down as well, Mr Java hands out cigarettes to warm up cold noses. Red Greek lips kiss the cigarette paper. Coughing, Mr Java leads the way through the loose sand; the captain gives him a friendly pat on the back.

Are they walking to the hotel?

No, to his own house. Over the sandy cobblestones, wind at their back, sand swirling around them. And talking English the whole time. The boy follows silently, looking around now and then to see what the village makes of it. Nothing. No one's watching. There goes his secret, won over by an excited Mr Java. God, what a racket he's making. His words splutter all over her coat. But she belongs to him. Don't they see that? In between all the English, she is really looking at him . . . They talk the language of eyes. He will now stick this woman in his album.

Their eye language doesn't last long. Mr Java slows his pace and sends the boy on ahead to warn Mother and the girls.

—

Panic in the house. Protests. Stamping girls' feet. All the same the kettle goes on for tea and a bucket of bleach is flushed down the loo and they dive into their wardrobes in search of something simple to wear. The poor Greeks, it wouldn't do to show them up.

Mother and the girls receive them in old slacks and pullovers, dressed for storm and shipwreck. They are visibly shocked when the woman takes off her coat. (In the kitchen Mother calls her 'Miss Elegance'.) But the captain is perfectly charming. He's called Homeros and, what can she say, Miss Elegance exceeds all expectations as well. She asks them to call her Ephtheia. The boy is unimpressed . . . she'd already written her name on the edge of the newspaper in her cabin, for him alone. Ephtheia does her trick for the girls now as well: she writes Greek letters in their school diaries and a line from the *Odyssey* for first sister to show round at school. They sniff with pride and there's no more mention of exam week.

Over the mulled wine, which was actually meant for Christmas, Ephtheia recites the Greek alphabet. What a show-off. Homeros sings a song and throws his arms around the girls.

They set up the table-tennis table. And open the tin of apricots. Cigarettes are passed around, without a tax label. Homeros pulls a hip flask out of his inside pocket – real Russian vodka! Mr Java has to taste it, filthy stuff from the look on his face, but after a few sips his cheerfulness knows no bounds. Into the kitchen to put on some rice, spices out of the cupboard, and in no time the whole house smells of pepper gardens and tobacco. Yes, Ephtheia and Homeros can look at the photo album . . . Middle sister tries on Ephtheia's stilettos, third sister holds up her diamond earrings and wants pierced ears on the spot. Glenn Miller comes out of his cover. For a moment it's quiet in the house, Mother wipes away a tiny tear . . .

It goes on like that for hours. With tiddlywinks, pick-up-sticks and goose – which proves impossible to explain. *Wonderful family*, say the guests. They never get round to Russians, immigration countries, safe havens or holes in the Iron Curtain. The atlas stays on the shelf, the boy doesn't have to turn on his globe. No plates or glasses get broken.

They forget to send the boy to bed. He keeps so quiet, even Ephtheia hardly notices him, now and then a distracted caress in passing. *Naughty boy*. She is going to London, she says, as soon as they get the ship free.

'*Oh, London.*'

'*Yes, London.*'

He hates English.

Wonderful family. What stupid people, these so-called foreigners. He hates them. He hates family. Is this actually his family? A mother who bends over backwards and pulls all kinds of delicacies out of the cupboard, Mr Java with his stories and funny faces, begging for a compliment from the captain, the girls with their phoney English. It's like . . . yes, what is it like? A family from a picture book, a family on the radio: the kind that call each other 'darling' and 'dearest' in radio plays, a terribly sociable family that sing on their way to the playground, whose every day is a delight. Do they even exist?

—

The next afternoon, when the low wintry light makes the stiletto dents in the brown lino look like craters and Mr Java has thoroughly erased all other traces of the visitors with mop and beeswax, the boy decides not to ride his bike past the *Katingo* after school. He'll never go again, he too has been marked! But in the middle of the night there's no getting out of it: someone raps on the window, someone rings the doorbell . . . Mr Java is standing next to his bed, 'Get dressed, quick! They're refloating the *Katingo*.' The whole village has turned out. And that at one o'clock at night. Mother and the girls are running around in trousers and pullovers. Half asleep, the boy steps into his boots and shuffles out. The girls clamp him between them and hurry him along, 'Run.' Their pullovers still smell of cigarette smoke. The wind has settled. It's snowing.

Snowflakes drift over the boulevard and it's strangely quiet, despite the crowd that has gathered. Everyone is looking the same way, at the black sea. There she goes, sliding almost imperceptibly into the water . . . Do they see her, or not? Suddenly she has disappeared into the darkness . . . without a farewell, without a blast of her horn.

They stand there among the villagers, huddled together. For a long time they look out to sea. The boy too.

The herring man has stayed at his post. Two gleaming kerosene lanterns illuminate his brand-new stall. Paid off from pea soup in less than a month. Mr Java treats from the housekeeping purse and Mother doesn't mind.

'What a rush all of a sudden,' says Mr Java after the first slurp. The whole family feels abandoned.

—

181

Another day later the boy sees the postman pedalling into the wind on the boulevard. He too stops to look at the channels on the beach – the suction dredger has wreaked havoc. 'I've got a package for you,' the postman tells him, 'the captain left it with the pilot in the rush. Asked if I could drop it off some time.' For him? 'No, for your parents.' A carton of American cigarettes and a bottle of French perfume, with a decorative bow and a card for *the wonderful family*. No paper seals. 'Contraband,' according to the postman. He looks crestfallen . . . they could have thought of him as well . . . after all those . . . 'Once I even took them soup on board.'

The boy gives him half the carton. He divides the rest between the five other newspaper boys – proud smokers one and all. In a quiet moment he flushes the perfume down the toilet. Refills the empty bottle with water. Card and bow carefully back in place. The girls wear it for days on end.

the world in colour

A cardboard tube steps into the room, the size of a rolling pin. The coat that is carrying the tube under one arm smells of cigars and coal fumes. Mr Java has made a long train journey and brings the smells of the compartment into the sitting room with him. The family wouldn't have smelt them if he hadn't rushed in so overwrought, his shirt stuck to his chest, panting and shouting, 'You have to see this.' 'Take your coat off first,' says Mother, who blows out the candle under the teapot, suddenly bad-tempered because she'd been enjoying the peace and quiet. Mr Java waves his tube around. No, his coat's staying on, his hat's staying on, guess what's in the tube first. He drums on the cardboard . . . he makes Mother listen to a soft, mysterious rustling. The girls come closer inquisitively, the boy tries to read the label, Mother slides her chair back and starts clearing up. 'No, wait, you'll never believe this,' says Mr Java. 'I've been to the inventors' fair . . .'

'You were supposed to go for a medical.'

'Medical science can't match this.' Mr Java isn't letting anyone spoil his fun. 'It was an opportunity I had to take.'

'You're all sweaty,' says Mother.

Mr Java shakes off his coat, the sleeve comes down over the tube.

'*S-h-e-e-t,*' the boy spells out loud.

'An American invention, not yet released for retail,' says Mr Java. A thick sheet of plastic sighs out of the tube, but once it's unrolled it contains the rainbow. Mr Java holds the screen up in front of his face: nose, lips and teeth are suddenly orangey red, as if he's bleeding out of his mouth; in the middle of his head his face shines blue; above that there's a yellow glow. And look, his white shirt has turned brown . . . Huh, when the screen moves, it flicks to green.

'And?' asks Mr Java.

'Put it away, you'll give us nightmares,' says Mother.

The boy jumps around him, he wants to look through the sheet as well . . . Gee, you should see this: an orange biscuit tin, brown teapot . . . and Mother's got blue hair. Mr Java turns the plastic around and Mother turns green, the teapot turns blue, the girls turn orange . . . A little higher and more of an angle and the colours change again.

'What is it?' asks Mother.

'Colour television,' says Mr Java. 'You just stick it on the tube.'

'But we don't have a television.' The girls roar with laughter.

Mr Java rolls the screen up carefully.

'And we have to economise!' says first sister.

'This sheet didn't cost me a penny, it was a free extra,' says Mr Java.

'With what?' asks Mother.

'The television.'

The table falls silent.

'We have to monitor the situation . . .' The Situation is his hobby, everyone in the village knows that. No one is better prepared for World War III. Since the first reports of the Russian H-bomb test, three years ago now, he hasn't been idle. He has dug out the cellar, stocked up enough tinned food for years and filled the preserving jars. The sandbags are still empty, but he has two shovels ready to excavate the garden. Civil Defence holds him up as an example! Half of the housekeeping money goes on the Situation and now this . . . a television. The girls look at each other in total disbelief. 'Television?' Really? Really! The boy dances around Mr Java. TV, TV. The first in the building. The first in the street. He would never have to visit drooling Ronnie again on Saturday and

Wednesday afternoons when half the village went to the retarded boy's house to watch TV . . . if you got a chance to see anything more than the back of his wedge-shaped head, because Ronnie always sat right in front of the screen, a couple of inches from the glass . . . The boy wants to run out straight away to tell everyone. 'When, when?' he asks.

'Tomorrow,' says Mr Java.

'Tomorrow never comes,' snaps Mother.

'Today,' says Mr Java, 'but they're delivering it tomorrow.'

'Stick to radio and newspaper.'

'No,' Mr Java says fiercely. 'I want to see those crooks move for once, not black and white, but colour, like the real world.'

'The world through a kaleidoscope,' says Mother.

—

The next afternoon a luxury delivery van pulls up in front of the house. The driver unloads a big box. The side of the box shows a picture of a fat little man, legs spread, wearing a bright blue suit and with a bald pink head, holding a television set in his upraised arms. The little man grins: this way up. The driver looks a lot grumpier: he pants and lugs the box along behind Mr Java . . . through a cluttered hall, past bikes and mopeds, and accompanied by lots of watch-the-wallpapers and careful-of-the-paints. It's not easy to find a good place for the set – out of the sunlight yet close to a power point and an easy chair – but after sliding around enough furniture Mr Java clears a spot near the window. The sitting room has been turned half upside-down. They still need a table, but for now the neighbours have offered them a tea chest.

Unpacking is a quiet moment. The girls aren't back from school, Mother says she has better things to do; that leaves Mr Java and son to witness the driver cutting the little man up with his knife. Beheaded, blue suit in ribbons, grin shredded . . . The outside of the box weeps, but the inside provides consolation: never before has so much splendour been displayed on a tea chest. Wood, glass, buttons . . . top quality – even without a picture, it's a feast for the eyes. While Mr Java caresses his acquisition with a duster, the driver fetches an iron H from the van and climbs up on to the roof with it, trailing a cable with two wires behind him. That's the antenna. The man shouts, screams, Mr Java hangs out of the window and follows instructions: turn the dial, no, the other one, shake the wire, turn the plug the other way . . . Snow, that's all the antenna gets out of the air. After lots of turning and adjusting, and climbing up on to the roof and back down again three times, the driver manages to get a test pattern. Black, white and grey squares and circles fan past, fall over, dribble from top to bottom, until finally he gets them sharp and stationary. The American sheet goes on the front and the test pattern takes on bright colours. Now they just have to wait for movement. There'll be a broadcast in the evening.

—

The girls have raced through their homework and set the chairs out ready, the overhead light is off and they've followed the instructions by leaving a small lamp on behind the television set. Everyone is sitting there ready, except for Mother who has left for the bedroom with her sewing-box. The TV is so hot that Mr Java has already had to Sellotape the plastic sheet three times, but now it stays put. The news can start! A violet glow colours the room. A gong sounds. Too hard. The news gets the shakes. The set hasn't played up like this before. When Mr Java takes a step forward to intervene, the picture steadies before he's touched a single dial. But the moment he sits down again, it resumes shivering. Sitting is shivering, standing is steady. So Mr Java watches standing. He's in the way like that so the girls stand up too. The boy looks for a place between eight legs . . . But they are rewarded, the news is very special: a dark-green ship sails right through the desert. An orange desert. Mr Java and the girls slide closer together, pointing at the great emptiness in the little box beneath them. A wisp of yellow sun breaks through the blue sky. The camera flies over water and sand . . . and what's that? Pyramids, yes, that's the Pyramids. Orange-red Pyramids. Like glowing coals behind a mica plate.

'But in real life they're brown,' says middle sister, who sailed past them.

Mr Java and the girls start bickering: no, impossible, they can't have seen Pyramids then. Desert, yes, for days on end, and the Red Sea. 'And that wasn't even coloured.'

'It's because of the sunset,' says Mr Java.

'It's broad daylight.'

Meanwhile, on the news, a ship is sinking in the Suez Canal. And another. Iron cadavers block the passage. Mr Java and the girls don't notice, they're quarrelling about the colours of sand, stone and pipelines, and about the palm trees . . . also orange. It's completely screwy as far as the girls are concerned. Apart from the throng of people down on the docks, they were small and brown like that. Egyptians . . . That's something they all agree on. The Egyptians wave at the camera. The girls wave back and smile at them, wonderful . . . That's it, that's what it was like, just as they remember it. Mr Java feels dizzy and raises his hands to his head, he sinks back on to his chair. 'They're coming very close.'

The weatherman's map shakes under the sleeve of his coat. Holland is green and brown, colours you can count on.

189

—

Two days later the family is sitting in position for the news again, still without Mother – she's on strike. The gong, the voice and some more fighting. Bombs from the sky, torpedoes through the water. Mr Java has struck it lucky, he's glowing. Now that he's read all the papers, he understands what he saw last time. 'The Brits have been caught with their pants down,' he says. But the Brits on the news are wearing overalls and leather jackets. Pilots. Orange teeth smile recklessly at the camera, or green or blue . . . depending on how high the aircraft carrier is riding the waves. Planes take off, planes descend. There are more descending than ascending, they dive, tumbling out of the rainbow by the dozen. The girls scream . . . Relax, it's the picture. The TV is dribbling. Yet again.

'The thing's broken,' says first sister.

Mr Java knows better. 'It's those bunglers at the news.'

It's all too much. Mother sends Mr Java to bed with a cup of sedative tea.

The next day the boy scans the grey sky over the sea in search of white lines and signals from pilots in distress.

—

The TV seems to be given over to misery, as if the devil's laughing up his sleeve: three times a week they broadcast the TV news and three times a week

190

they show pictures of war and crises. Gloomy ministers gather at emergency meetings, the queen requests a briefing, housewives stock up on candles and kerosene ('Too late, too late,' crows Mr Java), the news-readers have swapped their smiles for long faces. Right after the weather report they have to turn it off to let out a sigh and discuss it all. No matter how much the boy begs for a quarter of an hour of quiz — it teaches him so much and it's so good for his general knowledge — Mr Java thinks it's bad taste to watch a quiz when the Free West is under attack, no matter how big the prizes. 'It doesn't teach you a thing,' says Mother, not with all those quizzes and definitely not with all that fighting. 'It only makes us poorer. Anyway, who's paying for all this misery?'

'The Russians,' Mr Java says darkly, moving his sombre gaze away from the TV to stare out of the window instead.

'I mean, who's paying for the idiot box,' says Mother, pointing at the TV. She suspects that a bill has arrived (a company name she didn't know on an envelope). She laid it next to Mr Java's plate. 'These are special times,' he says when the girls ask him about it.

———

Mr Java has discovered something new. In his attempts to get his set to stop dribbling, he climbed up on to the roof himself and, while turning and testing, happened to pick up Germany. He hadn't even known it was possible. And the stuff they broadcast! War and more war, starting in the afternoon! Old wars and new wars, close and far away. The boy has to come and watch too: books and exercise books to one side, lessons from the news are lessons for life. Pay attention. See that grin, that's the grin of an occupier planting his flag on other people's property. The greasy smile of a pig-faced Russian. Their tanks advance on all sides, surging over fields, ploughing across ancient squares, church towers fall like trees in a storm. Soon they'll be at the border ... they've already taken Budapest. But look: the women of Budapest smear liquid soap on the streets, the Russian tanks spin on the bridges. Soap can change the course of history, one dollop is enough ... When a tank slides into the river, Mr Java cheers and praises the women's savvy. They know 'soap can win a war.' And what are the men of Budapest doing? The men are being hanged. Waiting for the noose with dignity, in long overcoats. Mr Java and the boy watch it happen, the German goes in one ear and comes out the other, but what flashes in through their eyes, that stays there. No matter how much the antenna makes it snow.

Mr Java will support the Hungarians, he'll donate money, buy even more beans, and tubs of liquid soap. He swears it on his knees in front of the TV. You couldn't drag him away from the screen. Sunglasses on – no one's allowed to see his tears.

Nonsense, where'd they get that idea? Sunglasses on, because of the glare from the snow.

—

The children's programmes don't stand a chance at home, the state of the world demands Mr Java's full attention – he has tied a cord to the H on the roof so he can search for flakes of Germany from the ground. The boy now has to choose between Mr Java's hot head and a view of the back of crazy Ronnie's.

The world is burning on all fronts. In Indonesia they're throwing out the last Dutchmen. Indonesia – a name Mr Java can hardly bring himself to say (at home, at the table, it's a forbidden word). He doesn't like using the old name, the Indies, either. The sound alone is so painful and he doesn't want to moan . . . No, he prefers to talk about 'the tropics', 'overseas' or just 'the old days'. But the pictures from the country of his birth on the news obliterate his memories of the old days: neglected botanical gardens, overgrown plantations, squares full of jeering Indonesians demanding the death penalty for a Dutch businessman and buildings smeared with slogans and skulls: KILL THE DUTCH. With all his headpower, these are images he could never have imagined. And the boy can't believe his eyes either: the whole photo album has been set in motion, even if the houses behind the plastic sheet aren't white, but blue and green and orange . . . The women are just as beautiful and the servants helping them pack their bags are as servile as ever . . . But these people aren't travelling for their pleasure, they're fleeing. Eurasians who, in the confusion, no longer know which country they belong to. People hoot at them on the streets, they hurry up the gangplank of a ship. Mothers with children wave at the quay, pressed up against the railing, staring at the palmy shore they are leaving behind. 'Twerps!' Mr Java shouts at them. 'You should have known better than to trust Monkey.'

———

Monkey. The nightmare personified. He too appears on the news. As large as life. Monkey, who is in the papers every day. With that inevitable black flowerpot on his head, his film-star sunglasses, his shoes with raised heels, his well-tailored suit. There he is . . . taking the salute from a military parade. 'On a gilded throne,' according to Mr Java, who describes what he sees at the top of his voice, in many more colours than the plastic sheet has to offer. The boy knows Monkey from hundreds of stories. Monkey is the man who brought disaster on Mr Java and his family, he's a thief, a traitor and a dreamer, an idiot, a dandy, a dictator. Mother doesn't approve of calling him Monkey, even if she can't bear the sight of him, and the girls are embarrassed when Mr Java rages over him like this, they just call him –

No, Mr Java doesn't want to hear it.

His real name must not be spoken in his presence. Monkey, neither more nor less. His photo in the paper meets with howls of derision, his ugly mug is discussed in detail. Monkey the polygamist. Monkey the civil engineer. Monkey the thief. Finally he lands in the rubbish bin, crumpled and spat upon. Or worse: cut up and lit with a match, so he'll curl up in the ashtray like a spider monkey – but that *really* was going too far for Mother. Say *Monkey* and there's no stopping Mr Java.

But the longer Monkey walks around there, in that box, on the tea chest, in colour and sound, the quieter Mr Java grows. He follows him open-mouthed. Down the aircraft steps, into the limousine. Every movement, every action . . . He almost creeps into the screen next to him. The boy sees the similarities between them. They have the same rolling gait – foot to the left, foot to the right – the same gestures, the same accent, smile, sunglasses. They both have good manners: ladies first and kiss their hands. He has an excellent tailor, shirt cuffs peek out from under his coat . . . Yes, Mr Java has to give him that. Apart from those funny flaps on his pockets, with the gold buttons.

Monkey has been on a world trip for months. In China he drinks tea with Mao Tse-tung . . . Bloody hell, Monkey is an honoured guest. This is better than the newspaper! The girls creep in from the dishes, Mother wrings her hands behind Mr Java's chair. Monkey hops from country to country . . . Visiting the Krauts, the Swiss, the pope, whose ring he kisses . . . That's going too far for Mother, she averts her eyes. But they pop back out of her head when Monkey walks hand in hand with Khrushchev, in the snow on the Kremlin.

'He's got a nerve,' whisper the girls.

Mr Java pants, it's all going too fast: Monkey gives a speech in America, of all places. The land of the liberators! Monkey speaks some spicy English.

'Listen to him!'

'The lip on the man!'

'Gracious.'

'*Purrrrerpp* . . .' A burp, a fart, howls of derision . . .

Monkey is buried under confetti – a tickertape parade. Look at him lap it up! The camera is at his feet, his jaw swells with applause. Boy Scouts wave flags. Monkey gets bigger and bigger and, in the sitting room, as they watch, they get smaller and smaller . . . The boy sees his family shrink, even though Mr Java is still standing to keep the picture under control. Monkey on staircases, steps and stages, waving his field marshal's baton. And walking next to him, like a little shadow, a brown-skinned boy in a magnificent suit. The brown-skinned boy, too, looks up to Monkey.

'He's got his son with him,' Mr Java says with surprise.

'Whose is that one?' asks Mother.

Men in dark suits bow to welcome Monkey's son. He shakes President Eisenhower's hand, inspects the guard of honour, rows of decorated soldiers salute him, a boy! He gets to sit in the cockpit of a jet fighter, they put a helmet on his head. A son without a trace of doubt, his feet are used to red carpets.

The boy commits the monkey son to memory, he studies his gait and smile, he measures his suit from top to bottom, he estimates him to be the same height as himself, maybe even the same age . . . He wants clothes like that too. He would like to look up to a father as well . . . He tries . . . But Mr Java is too angry. It's beyond him.

'Monkey see, monkey do,' says Mother.

Even before the presenter (another red dog) has had time to announce the rest of the evening's programme, Mr Java switches off. 'He's playing them off against each other,' he says. This time he doesn't walk to his regular spot in front of the window, but rummages among the empty flowerpots behind the curtain on the windowsill. He blows the dust out of a pot, puts it on his bald head, sunglasses on, and turns back to the room with a teeth-baring grin and a torrent of incomprehensible words . . . Monkey-style, *ac*centu-ating all the wrong syl*lab*les. It's his own accent. Mr

Java is Monkey.

Mother and the girls scream with laughter. Fists in their crotches, they can't take it any more. Funnier than TV, they all say.

—

'We'll be bankrupt by the end of the month,' Mother warns the next evening, looking askance at the TV.

'The month's just started,' Mr Java says. 'You don't know what will happen.'

'There's been a letter waiting for you for days.'

'The whole world is waiting.'

Mother walks over to the desk, waves the envelope threateningly. 'Now,' she says. 'Now,' the girls shout.

'Think of your mother,' Mr Java says under his breath.

The letter-opener cuts through the paper . . . Mother's eyes say more than enough: she tosses the letter on to the table. The girls flock in on it. They read open-mouthed. 'What does hire purchase mean?' asks third sister. 'It's already a month behind,' says middle sister. 'Second instalment in three weeks,' says first sister.

'We're not keeping it,' Mother announces. Mr Java blows a piece of fluff off the plastic sheet. 'You hear me?'

'No.'

—

'That box isn't doing us any good,' says Mother and she's not the only one who thinks so. Dr Kofferman (the psychiatrist who is advising her), the chemist (who sells her calming herbs), the girls — they all agree. She's at the end of her tether, she can't take any more, doesn't anyone spare *her* a thought? They've struck bottom, of the housekeeping purse especially. She looks worried, she sounds worried.

And Mr Java? He's having a ball, watching the showjumping. It's beautiful. Horses float over green hedges. Clods of earth fly through the air. Westphalian greys, Arabians, Lipizzaners, standard-breds. And a cloud-free sky with the sun shining, the way it should. For the first time the colours are right: brown on the ground, green for things that grow low, reddish for things that are moving and above it all a rainbow of colours with plenty of blue and violet. The world under control. Showjumping for ever, no more war.

A luxury delivery van pulls up, a man climbs out and unloads a big box. The box bounces on the ground, the man pulls it along behind him with one hand. It is an empty box. On the side there is a picture of a fat little man, legs spread, arms raised, in a bright blue suit; his face has been torn away, his hands cut off. The driver looks sullen. Mother waits for him in the hall. She whispers, showing the man where to get the ladder. He takes the H down from the roof and rolls up the antenna wire. Inside Mr Java is watching the showjumping in the snow . . . falling riders, dribbling horses . . . he has put on his sunglasses. He doesn't put up any resistance when the TV disappears into the box – right side up. It is a quiet moment. Mother and the man talk about instalments. After the van has driven off, Mr Java draws the heavy curtains – no reason to let everyone see that the violet glow has suddenly disappeared from the sitting room. He doesn't take off the sunglasses. He's had enough of colour. And doesn't need to see the red on his son's cheeks.

the plunge

The Brits have shipped ninety-three tanks to Suez, the crates with the officers' silverware and the champagne are waiting for onward transport from the docks of Port Said, the French have called up their reservists and what does the government do in The Hague? The Hague rolls over in bed . . . Not Mr Java, he tunes in to the BBC in the middle of the night, he doesn't miss a thing, he's ready. He's inspected the cellar, replenished the stocks, sealed off cracks and chinks in the house. And he hasn't forgotten the lifeboat horses. They are sensitive creatures and smell danger before people have the slightest suspicion. Every day he goes out riding on a different horse – the fitter they are, the more you can count on them in an emergency. Sometimes he lets all eight out on the beach. They trot around and splash in the sea, but when they've had their run they line up in front of him as a team. Rows of four. He looks on contentedly: they're so obedient and strong . . . if only everyone had their affairs in such good order.

When the weather report announces a strong easterly and Mother hears that strange sound again – the ruffling hoofs come back after a long absence – Mr Java goes straight to the stable. It all seems quiet. But the wind swings round that evening to blow from the north-west, and the following morning from the north-east. The swirling wind pushes the sea up against the land and waves pound the coastal strip. There are reports that the water is washing over the sea wall a little further north. Mr Java feels that the horses feel something . . . but what? 'Maybe they want to finally prove themselves.'

'So they're longing for a shipwreck,' says middle sister.

How can she say that? They just want to show their strength . . . Who doesn't, in times like these?

—

That second day Mr Java had already been to the stable a couple of times and after dinner the boy had to go with him. Under protest, as always. The horses might have a good nose for fallout . . . but that evening *he* smelt *their* cold sweat, they stunk worse than ever, despite the wind whipping through the stable. He refused to go in. That's what he says the next morning, when the people in the village have joined together to search for words to make a single story of all that has happened in the night. Because it's too much . . . nobody can grasp it alone.

The boy comes riding up on his bike when the excitement is at its peak . . . a day to bunk off school. Everyone is talking at once. Everyone expected an alarm: the lifeboat crew (the boy had watched them for a while, scraping algae off the hull so they could launch a smooth boat), the people who always show up on the boulevard when it's blowing a gale, and had therefore turned out again that night, a few beach fishermen and Pickle the beachcomber. And the bell rang: a ship in trouble. The neighbouring villages of Egmond and Petten had been alerted as well. They hitched the horses in front of the boat, with Mr Java helping. Sipstein, from the lifeboat service, says that they all had a good laff about that East Indian bloke (Mr Java) who was way too dressed up while uz lot (the volunteers) were slitherin' round in the algae. And that Mr Java had slipped over in his best clobber and whacked his head on the boat. 'Maybe that put the wind up the horses. Anyroad he went all woozy and his son took him home to their lodgings (the family home).'

The boy thinks it's nice of Sipstein not to publicly call Mr Java 'the Indo', the way the volunteers usually do . . . but he soon realises that it's not about Mr Java at all (even though the bump on his head kept the family busy all night). It's much worse.

Pickle the beachcomber says it was the hand of God. The carpenter claims nothing like this would have happened with a tractor. 'That's obvious,' counters someone else, 'with a tractor there wouldn't've been any horses.' But it wasn't in any way the fault of those poor horses: everyone, except Pickle, is agreed on that score. They were such beautiful animals . . . But how did it happen?

'They suddenly fell away,' says Sipstein, 'just after the launch, a few steps into the breakers, big waves, but not too big, we were just pickin' up speed, about to uncouple and . . . there they went, before yer very eyes – whoosh to the bottom. As if they'd been chucked off a cliff. Too shocked to swim – straight into the deep. The waves turnin' over their heads. They came this close to takin' uz with 'em.'

The boy can't believe his ears.

'But it's not deep there,' a fisherman shouts, 'you could stand there.'

'It only come up to my hip where we went in,' says Sipstein. 'One of the men went in first with a sounding rod . . . we always do that.'

'We weren't looking that way neither,' another volunteer backs up Sipstein, 'we was scanning the waves for the ship, my eyes was fixed on a light bobbing in the distance. We didn't actually see nothing.'

Measurements are taken and heads are shaken . . . and to think it was a false alarm all along . . . they could just as well have stayed on shore. The ship saved itself.

It's terrible.

The wife of the owner of the butter factory, whose house looks out over the beach, asks, 'Could it be because of that suction dredger? When they were trying to dislodge that Panamanian freighter they made some very deep trenches there.' The Panamanian freighter, that was such a long time ago . . . No, no one made any connection there. Except Pickle, he says the beached ship was a plague on the village, because the Lord –

'Because there was nothing for you to steal,' a brash Egmonder shouts him down.

And the people stood there like that for a long time, discussing things, trying to imagine in words what could have happened that night.

—

Mr Java only heard it on the radio around midday and walked to the beach at once – reeling down the street against medical advice, because he'd been ordered to rest in bed in the dark for at least a week. For hours he stood staring into the waves, until Mother came to fetch him back. At home he doesn't want to talk about it. With a show of complete calm he even manages to comfort the boy . . . *his* horses won't end up as smoked sausage. As soon as they wash up, he'll see to it that they get a grave in the dunes.

But the horses don't wash up. It's not until a few days later that the drama becomes visible, at ebb on a sunny day, after the storm has died down. The sand-bars are exposed and glittering between them are deep dark trenches. What used to be wadable sea is now a grave for eight Zeeland lifeboat horses.

Mr Java doesn't want to go and look, he prefers to stay in the darkness of his bedroom, where he has already seen his faithful team two nights running: next to his bed in two rows of four.

When Mother hears that she immediately goes to the milkman to call Dr Kofferman.

the hare

The Royal Mail has delivered the hare, the annual Christmas gift from the tenant. A stiff dead hare in its winter coat with a label round its neck. And now it's hung up waiting to be skinned. And every year the question's the same: who is going to do it? Mother again? Cold-blooded slaughter runs in her family, Grandfather kills chickens by jabbing a darning needle into their brains. But this time she can't bring herself to do it. 'As far as I'm concerned we can celebrate a vegetarian Christmas this year.' Anyway, she says, she always did it more for the fur than the meat. And the whole family is already fitted out with hare-skin mittens.

Mr Java then? Up till now he's done a good job of shirking. 'There are some things you shouldn't be able to do. Butchering is for the staff.'

The girls? In a pinch they can skin snakes and roast monkeys – learnt it all in the camp. But a putrid hare? No!

'It's supposed to be like that,' Mother says, 'it's game.'

Game or no game, they're not playing along.

Bury it then?

Vetoed by Mr Java. 'We are not, under any circum-
stances, throwing away food.'

Mother has a better idea. 'This year we'll ask a
labourer.' There's a building site just up the road and
quite a few 'he-men' walking around.

'What am I supposed to be, a she-man or something?' asks Mr Java. Ever since Mother accidentally
accused him of fussing like a hen during one of his
cleaning fits, this has been a delicate subject.

'Working men are less sensitive,' Mother explains.

Mr Java is not having it. 'Sharpen the knives!'

—

The hare is on the worktop. Mr Java has put on an
apron. Mother and the girls hurry to the sitting room.
The boy hesitates on the threshold between kitchen
and hall and watches out of the corner of one eye.
Of course, it's only a question of headpower. Mr Java
can do it. He can already see the pieces of dressed
meat in the frying pan. He just has to get rid of the
skin and innards. A nick here, a nick there, teeth
clenched . . .

'When is that bloody tenant going to stop treating
us to a half-rotten cadaver every year?' grumbles Mr
Java. Mother has inherited a strip of field, so small
the rent is paid in kind. 'If you ask me he only does

it to annoy her, to remind her of the stench she fled.'
But Mr Java doesn't turn his nose up at a job like
this – gently, he will help the hare out of its coat. A
writer's hand does not eschew the knife.

There he goes . . . chin up, and a little slash on the
neck . . . The boy walks out of the kitchen. He hears
thuds on the worktop, a running tap, a curse, a cry
. . . The next time he peeks around the door, Mr Java
is covered with blood, a whole spray from stomach
to face. He hasn't noticed. With his eyes shut, he is
tugging on the hare's hairy head and its half-naked
back. The animal shivers in his hand. And crashes into
the sink. Blood and water splash up. A shocked Mr
Java looks at his hands. Red up to the wrists. He
walks into the hall, holding his arms out in front of
him, following those strange, dripping hands. A call
for help. Drops falling on the lino. Red fingerprints
on the doorpost. The boy walks along behind Mr
Java and can only see splashes. Mr Java comes to a
standstill in the middle of the room. He is crying.
'You do it,' he tells Mother. 'You grew up surrounded
by blood.'

She acquits herself of the task manfully. And gives
the boy a hare's foot for luck.

Christmas

Christmas Eve. Hare. A hare full of shot. Mr Java spits out four pellets, the girls five between them. Hard balls of lead, they rattle on the plates. Mother bites down on three and has swallowed two – it's hard for her to notice them with her false teeth. Lay the pellets on the side of the plate. That's how you do it. The boy uses his spoon to fish pellets out of the sauce. War crunches in the bottom of the dish. He's already got three. 'Funny kind of hunter, that tenant of yours,' Mr Java mumbles, 'it's enough to give you lead poisoning.' His knife slips, a pellet rolls over the floor. Overrrrrrr . . . the lino. He ignores it. Things like that can happen with a little ball like that.

A small, unimportant pellet.

But it bothers Mr Java. He looks under the table, under his chair, behind his back. Cheeky little pellet. You'd think it was already shot. Dead pellet. But it's got a mind of its own and rolls on. He's not shot of it yet. Down on his knees for a better look. Where's that bloody pellet? A fried, greasy pellet. It can't have rolled too far.

The family pull in their legs and give instructions. When Mr Java's chair remains embarrassingly empty, Mother gets down on the floor to keep him company. Then the girls too, and the boy: all on their knees searching the floor with the palms of their hands. Maybe under the rug, behind the leg of the sideboard? Mother bangs her head on the tabletop, tries to get up, thinks she's grabbed the leg of the table, but pulls the tablecloth instead. There goes the hare, the apple sauce, the mash and the sprouts, whooshing down a damask slide and into the sitting room . . . forks and knives bring up the rear, with the plates . . . and the pellets.

Mr Java wipes the shards aside and sticks to the job at hand. Where is his pellet?

Mother looks at the havoc and kneels again. 'Here's one.'

'No, that one just fell.' Mr Java wants his own pellet. His rolled more to the left.

'Is it this one then? Or this one?'

Impossible, he's already checked there twice.

'Here, this one's nice and round.'

'They're all round.'

'No, they're not. Feel it, this one's flat, a ricocheted pellet.'

Mother, the girls, the boy, they hold up every discovery: an apple seed from the sauce, a misplaced

211

grain of rice, a mouse poo that had been swept into the crack under the skirting board . . . anything that feels round and hard, but nothing is like that one Christmas pellet, cast off from his plate.

Something else rolls. A tear rolls down Mr Java's cheek. Yes, he has been a bit weepy lately. He crawls under the table, creeps into his coat . . . he shrinks. Mother passes him a serviette, but Mr Java swats her consolation away. He kicks out, a fork goes flying, big shards break into little shards. He grabs a piece of hare, that bloody hare, and hurls it at the wall . . .

The girls and the boy screw up their eyes, they know this sound. The pieces of the gravy boat, the pieces of a plate. Something new is the sound of broken crockery mixed with mash, they hardly ever eat potatoes, it's stickier. The wallpaper cries.

Mr Java cries.

Candles out. Pieces in the rubbish bin. And off to bed. Everyone off to bed. Mr Java will tidy up, by himself. No need to wash, and leave your socks on. Eight thirty. Christmas Eve.

———

The next morning the dining table is forbidden territory. Stay in your bedrooms! Mr Java is tidying up. It's not until midday – after the news – that the sitting-room door opens . . .

And isn't it pretty: Christmas paper on the breakfast table, red bells under the table lamp and a lovely smell of Christmas loaf and beeswax, glue, paint and bleach, but hasn't it taken a long time for it to smell so peaceful again?

No one cleans up the mess they make as well as Mr Java cleans up the mess he makes. Sweeping, mopping, scrubbing, touching up damage with paint, re-gluing torn wallpaper – he works his rage away and when he's finished he wipes it all with bleach. Bleach is his eau-de-Cologne, that's what really calms him down.

They're allowed to light the candles. A mandarin each is lying next to their plates. Silently Mother cuts the Christmas loaf, scared to death she'll slip with the knife. Nothing must happen to upset Mr Java. The family is playing merry Christmas. The girls bite their serviettes to smother their nervous giggles. The boy swallows a sneeze.

'I still owe you a Christmas story,' says Mr Java, 'we didn't get round to it last night. Listen:

'I had a riding friend, very popular at the show-jumping, owner of two magnificent racehorses and a tobacco plantation. Nice guy, honest, fair, loved by the natives. As bald as a billiard ball.'

The girls squeeze out their mandarin peel in front of the candles. The oil crackles in the flames.

'You want to hear it or not?'

More crackling.

'Anyway, my friend was already bald at twenty, maybe that's why he never married. At thirty he was still single. No, wait . . . I'm not doing him justice, he was smart, he had a good head – after all, it's the contents that matter. A man with a heart for his business, always coming up with his own inventions, importing the latest machines, building a school for the labourers' children. The war split us up. I had to think of him sometimes in those years when I heard the dying scream of a horse on the other side of the barbed wire . . . hunger brings out cruelty, yes . . . ah, he had magnificent thoroughbred Arabians. Then, one day, as luck would have it, I bumped into him again . . . no, it wasn't luck, we were out of luck, it was peace, but a terrible time, yes, rebellion, armed gangs, chaos, you didn't know where to go, travelling was dangerous and we were stuck in the area where my friend had his plantation, the European neighbourhoods were burning, the hinterland was smouldering and the tobacco wasn't what it used to be either . . .' Mr Java fell silent, staring into the flame of a candle.

'I was sitting there in my Red Cross rags and suddenly he rode past: proud, on horseback, in uniform, cavalry, just like me, I had never seen him so jaunty. How had he got a horse? "Confiscated," he said, "I took it back, actually." He had seen one of his old hands with it. It was his own horse, no question of that.'

'Is this going to be a horse story or a Christmas story?' asks Mother.

'Christmas was just around the corner – not that we celebrated it, the population was too busy with other gods and that handful of soldiers weren't bothered either, after all the wonderful things we'd been through, we'd had more than enough of the God of the Christians.

'My friend went out riding one day. Stupid . . . he knew that too, but he couldn't stand it any more. After all those rumours he wanted to know what was left of his business. On the way he bumped into a gang of men armed with sticks and guns. Rebels. One of them, the leader, asked where he was going. "To my plantation," my friend answered. "Ah, a planter," the fellow shouted, pressing his rifle against the horse's neck. But the others recognised him, the old ones, and a few youngsters, who'd worked for him or gone to his school. He was glad to see them, they were too . . . My friend dismounted to greet them – but the leader stepped between them. "Planter!" he screamed. "What's so special about a planter, why so much respect for this man? He's no more a planter than you are. You can plant too . . . it's your own land! This man is an enemy of the people. He made you suffer. Now he has to suffer."

He lashed out with the butt of his rifle and grazed my friend's bald head . . . stepped back and gestured to the other rebels . . . they could have their way with him. My friend wanted to jump back on his horse, but they had already grabbed the reins. He tried to run, taking cover behind a wall, but they dragged him out from behind it, beating him with sticks. They pulled him back up on to his feet, let him go again, caught up with him, and beat and kicked him again. The crowd following him grew. Until they passed a church. A priest came out to see what the racket was about. He wanted to help the planter and stepped between him and the raging mob. A woman came to help too, an old cook who recognised her former master: she tried to give him some water but a couple of young hotheads smacked the bottle out of her hands. "Kill the baldie!" they shouted. "And the priest with him." . . . Voices behind other people's backs, faceless voices . . .

'The priest managed to escape in the commotion, but my friend was dragged through the villages. He was groaning with pain. They let him come to under a tree, a nice tree to hang him from. They tested branches, tied his horse's reins around his neck and pulled them tight. Someone washed the blood from his face and wiped it out of his eyes, so he'd have a better view of his own hanging . . . we heard that later. He must have had hope even then, he was far from dead. He offered them money, they used it to buy food, stuffed his mouth full of rice, gave him a drink, then kicked him in the stomach to make him throw it all up again –'

'Lovely,' exclaims middle sister.

Mr Java isn't listening, he left the table long ago, he pulls his friend away from the evildoers, he's holding the reins in his hand, even if it's just a serviette: 'They dragged him past houses and huts, and more and more people joined the mob.' His voice gets hoarser and hoarser. 'They walked along behind, or rode bikes, most of them didn't even know what it was about. A planter who had done something wrong – drunk, no doubt – seduced a young girl maybe . . . things like that happened. And he apparently shouted, "Long live the queen." "Long live the queen?" "*Republik, republik,*" chanted overgrown youths. "*Merdeka!*" New voices, new tormentors. Villagers joined the throng, others wandered off . . . In the end no one had done anything, no one was guilty. It rained stones, sticks lashed down. It went on like that for two hours. His head was a bloody ball. "Should we shoot you or beat you to death?" an old peasant asked. "Shoot," he begged, "shoot." "Do you hear that?" shouted the peasant. "Get your guns." But the people just stood there. They wanted him to suffer . . . suffer before their eyes.'

'That's enough,' Mother says firmly. She can see the boy soaking it all up.

217

'It wasn't enough for my friend's persecutors,' Mr Java snaps at her. 'The kicking, beating and stoning went on. All respectable men, as it turned out later. Not even that young: fathers of children, grandfathers too, there was a trishaw rider, a stringy little fellow in his sixties, he laid in with a bicycle chain . . . A Christian convert, I heard later. And when my friend was lying there like a corpse, the children lent a hand. They dipped their sticks in his blood. One fourteen-year-old boy challenged another.

'"What? You too scared? Chicken! You haven't got any blood on your stick." They wanted to set fire to him, to roast him, to eat him up.

'"Now the priest," the adults shouted, "let's burn them both and lay one at right angles over the other, together they'll make a nice cross!" Amen,' says Mr Java and he pokes his serviette through the ring.

Mother scrapes the mandarin peel together and piles up the plates. 'You call that a Christmas story?'

'It happened at Christmas.'

Rosehill

Bag packed, coat brushed, he's counted his money,
his worries, Mother's worries. Mr Java is ready. He
looks at his watch, counts, that damned counting
again – something recent. He walks over to the
window. There goes the baker in his little grey van,
cigar in mouth, hair white from the flour. Messy. No,
not with the baker. The local train? Doesn't run in
the winter – not enough passengers.

'Eat some soup first,' Mother says, 'it will be a cold trip.'

Soup?

Her eyes beg.

Mr Java has to get his strength up, he has hurled his
dinner at the wallpaper so many times that his cheek-
bones are sticking out like shards now as well. 'Yes,
yes, bring on the soup,' he mumbles to himself. Soon
he'll get bad food. Institutionalised soup, thin and
watery. Bring it on.

Mr Java eats his soup. The family nods along with
every spoonful.

Dr Kofferman rings the bell. He drags his feet, that's what you get with a name like that.

'Doctor, if I don't want to, I don't have to, do I?' asks Mr Java.

'You're under no obligation,' says Dr Kofferman.

'Hear that?' Mr Java says to Mother.

'You don't have to, but the rest will do you good.' The doctor is on her side.

'Can my boy come with me?' Mr Java asks Dr Kofferman. They are going to Rosehill, the mental hospital. But he's not mad, he's just tired. 'I'm only going there to sleep, to sleep and sleep, the moment I get there, I'm going straight to bed . . . Why should I finish my soup?' His voice is hoarse.

The boy is allowed to accompany him to the gate – not inside, not yet.

Mr Java says goodbye. The girls are so close to their mother he can't get to her cheeks, they're protecting each other. He blows a kiss instead. 'Yes, goodbye, goodbye, OK. It's time to go now.'

There he goes down the garden path, between the boy and the doctor, he waves briefly and straightens his back to shrug off the neighbours' eyes. The boy feels them as well. They stare straight ahead.

Mr Java sits next to Dr Kofferman. The boy gets in

the back, with a view of two necks and two collars. The doctor's coat is sagging, his collar is crumpled and the edge of his tie is showing underneath, he needs a haircut. The doctor is a picture of calm. Mr Java sits up straight in his tweed, his collar is glistening with starch, his tie is knotted high, and his neckline and sideboards are neatly trimmed. With the reins pulled tight, he can't keep himself under control. He's always getting carried away with things, that's what Mother says.

You wouldn't think so . . . not from the restrained way he's sitting there and asking the doctor about the buttons and dials on the walnut dashboard, not from the calm with which he looks out of the side window and points out a hare on a dune. He waves at the hare. The hare stands up on its rear legs.

'You be careful now,' says Mr Java.

The hare laughs.

the first dance

First sister gnaws her pen and sweats over a letter to Mr Java:

It's my fault, I chose you, or was it the other way round? We chose each other, let's leave it at that. You, who in the last few years have taken to starting every story with 'in the old days', will no doubt remember different things, but I still have a very clear memory of how it started between us: with waiting, weeks of waiting, behind the closed gates of the evacuation camp, in a fenced-off part of the port area. Waiting for news and waiting for a ship and every day I saw you. You weren't like the other soldiers, you never wore your uniform. Now it's almost impossible to imagine. Did I know what I was looking for? And what were you after? You came to our barrack with me, saw our sick mother, found soap and pretty clothes for us. I got a white embroidered dress. You knew the holes in the fence, but remained proper and courteous. I have to give you that. The way you asked Mummy out, in a suit and tie . . . goodness, but she didn't dare. After the camp she collapsed completely. We had fought so hard to keep her going. It was touch and go. Women don't get medals, but she didn't deserve any either. In the camp I was often ashamed of her. Sometimes I can hardly believe my eyes when I see how strong she has become now. Strong next to you. She should be grateful. And not just for the medicine you managed to organise. What you don't know is that Mummy didn't think much of you at first. A rake, that's what she thought you were. How could a man pursue pleasure when every day people were being crossed off the list of the missing and added to the list of the dead? She was so scared of the future. She was embarrassed about her loose teeth and our ragged corner of the dormitory. But because you were so good to her — the mosquito net! — she let me go out for a walk with you. And we walked, on the missionary-post dance floor. My God, we must have been a sight. I was a skinny kid and you were a bag of bones and still we felt strong. We weren't looking back, you definitely weren't. My body had been at a standstill for years and suddenly I blossomed. Going to bed too late in the evening I saw Mummy's sighs rustling the curtain. She didn't complain, but the whole barrack felt sorry for her. Dabbing her forehead with cold rags, changing her bed, emptying the potty, helping her to the washroom . . . yes, that helped. Cinderella at Mother's bedside. The moment I pulled on my white dress, she started pining away. As far as that goes, you're like each other: being weak gives you power. When I see you two at it like this I can't help but think of our first weeks, although I try to shake it off. Sorry.

There's been more than enough whining about the old days at home, but there's one thing I've always wanted to ask. Was it politeness that made you ask Mummy out dancing?

Or was the pension of a first lieutenant's widow an attractive prospect . . . No, how vicious, you couldn't have known that then. When she had picked up a little she wanted to go out with you after all and it led to a real struggle before the mirror: she wanted to put on my white dress – she was skinny and vain enough – and if her belly hadn't been swollen from oedema it would have fitted her too. More and more widows dared to go out dancing. Even if we were still waiting for official notification about my father . . . but grief soon wears thin. You fitted together well, I saw that from the first tango. Hips at the same height, even if she was a good bit older than you. Leading and bleeding. And now the roles are reversed.

But don't forget, the first dance was mine.

———

The letter ends up in the bin.

visiting

The craziest thing about the crazies at Rosehill is
how normal they look, the boy noticed that the
moment he stepped into the glass lobby: respectably
dressed men walking around by themselves, it didn't
show at all. None of them were flapping six fingers,
frothing behind bars or claiming to be Napoleon . . .
they weren't sick on the outside. Lucky for him, that
meant no one could see he was the son of a lunatic.

Mother does think that the men she passes in the
long corridor have a very listless gait. She herself is
tense and strides out with her heavy basket filled with
snacks and clean clothes. Visiting patients in their
rooms is against the rules, but an exception is made
for sleepyheads like Mr Java. They don't see any
women on the way, but standing in front of his room
they hear a high female scream. 'I thought they had
separate departments,' Mother says anxiously. She
listens at the door and knocks.

It is only after some bumping around that Mr Java
opens the door, not in pyjamas but decked out in his
suit. He looks at Mother and the boy as if he hadn't

been expecting visitors. Mother steps into the small room shyly, forgetting to kiss him.

'You look nothing like I thought,' says Mr Java vaguely. 'Can't faces change a lot in three weeks.'

'You've changed.' Mother wants to kiss him after all, but he recoils. 'Your face has got fatter.'

'From the tablets and the injections.' And from the sleep, gosh, the whole first fortnight all he did was sleep.

His eyes are gentler, without the hard glare they had before Christmas, he seems to have shaved his temples higher and he looks pale; a melancholy smile plays on his lips. But he grins when Mother inspects his room: the undersized wardrobe, two high-backed chairs, a writing table, the sheets of the single bed, bedside cabinet, a radio . . . 'Is that allowed?' she asks, raising a finger.

'On loan from a kind-hearted nurse. You hear everything here, I turn it on to drown out the neighbours' voices.'

They unpack the basket: lots of brain food and a bottle of cream. ('Cream is goodness,' Mother has read somewhere.)

'No newspapers?'

'Oh, how silly of me . . . I forgot,' Mother says, looking at the boy out of the corner of her eye.

226

Mr Java checks the starch concentration in the collars of his shirts. The girls have sent their best wishes in letters and a home-made cake: it's exam week again. The boy didn't know what to give, he has brought his exercise book with him to show his progress in writing. He wants to sit down on the bed next to Mr Java and nestle up against him without a word, but Mr Java doesn't want to get too close. He doesn't want to shake hands or kiss. 'There are all kinds of bugs going round this place.'

While Mother packs the dirty laundry away and lays the clean shirts in the wardrobe, he leafs through the exercise book. He grumbles, groans, pulls his fountain pen out of his coat, crosses out and corrects. 'Look at these letters! Your loops have grown,' he says, 'you're turning them into lassos. You trying to rope someone?'

The boy looks uncomfortable.

'Here they catch patients with words. Be careful! You don't get out of those snares easily. The good doctors talk you into a disease, even if nothing's wrong with you. They measure you up for delusions and manias until you're ripe for a straitjacket. Yippee-aye-ay!' Mr Java flaps a piece of paper he's pulled out of his inside pocket. There's writing on it. 'I've collected a few of them for you: monomania, hypomania . . . Wait, I'll write them down for you, you can have some fun showing the kids at school.' The manias surge through his exercise book: 'Megalomania, trichotillomania . . .'

'Trick a what?' says Mother, with her head in the wardrobe.

'That's people who pull out their hair.' Mr Java taps his gleaming bald skull.

'Do you have them here?'

'We don't need any barbers, that's for sure. And poriomania . . . Now poriomania, that's a fabulous complaint. Poriomaniacs have to wander, going off in search of adventure every day, but they don't remember what they've experienced. Picture it – life as a photographer without a roll of film.'

'That's crazy,' Mother blurts out. 'All that learning for a few loonies.'

'Yes, we keep the good doctors busy,' Mr Java says, suddenly serious. 'But their words scare us. They're so informed: this is a curve and that's a corner and here's the start and there's the end. And when I say, "But doctor, when I get lost I see a lot more . . ." you hear the scorn in their voices. There's not a tree left can surprise them. Their jungle is called pill bottle. They cut people down to size and destroy everything.' Mr Java plays with the cap of his pen. 'Just the day before yesterday,' he says quietly to Mother, 'a fellow in his early thirties . . . it makes you wonder where he found the rope.'

'*Shhh*,' says Mother, 'not in front of the boy.'

228

But the boy hasn't been able to follow it for a long time now, he's still back at the lasso. He'd like to have one, a lasso to catch Mr Java and lead him away, far from all these dangerous men and manias.

Mother walks over to the narrow window that looks out on a dingy garden. 'And which word do they use for you?' she asks dully.

Mr Java doesn't see or hear, he is once again engrossed in his list: 'Megalomania, mythomania . . .'

'I thought you were only supposed to sleep here.'

The sleep therapy has been completed. Mr Java is still a bit drowsy, he says, but over the last week he's even been allowed to go for walks and the nurses have taken him out with them.

'Out?'

'To the dining hall, the craft centre, the conversation room.' Would they like to see his department?

Shall he give her a tour? He's suddenly acting cheerful again.

There's nothing Mother would rather do than get out of that stuffy room.

A little later the three of them are walking down the long high corridors. Mr Java slowly, Mother hurried, past doors and even more doors. Now and then she sighs and slows, looking up at the high grey ceilings

– unattainable heavens. They pass a door that's been kicked in. 'That's where they keep the nut smith,' Mr Java tells the boy.

'He's talking nonsense,' snaps Mother.

The corridor of doors comes out in a bright room. A semicircle of windows with a glass roof – there's no one there because it's visiting time. 'This is the conversation room,' Mr Java says.

Mother and the boy study the room. Coconut matting on lino, wooden table, pale chairs arrayed around it – all plain birch, including the newspaper box. 'Danish design, cold and sensible.' Mr Java strokes the back of a chair. 'How sad to live life as a Danish birch. First they stand there shivering in the Arctic wind in their silver skin, then they get sacrificed on the altar of seated discomfort . . . Look at how fine the grain is, they were cut down much too young. Arne Rasmussen is a bastard.'

'Who's Arne Rasmussen?' asks Mother.

'His name is under each chair.'

'But they're bright,' Mother soothes him, 'not gloomy.'

'The wood is weeping,' says Mr Java. 'Try sitting on it. If that doesn't make you sad . . .'

Mother tries a Danish chair. Feet wide apart.

'And?'

'Lovely.'

'Lovely! You never want to feel what I say.'

She presses her handbag down on her lap. 'What do you think?' She looks to the boy for support, but he's turned his head away and doesn't answer. He has suddenly discovered terrifying manias in the grain of the Danish table.

'You have an insensitive bum,' says Mr Java.

What a tone. Not another word about the chairs. Mother tries to find a different subject. 'It must be fascinating, having conversations in here.'

'Euchre and whist, yes. I refuse to sit here — those chairs are still growing,' says Mr Java.

'Yes, you've made your point!' screams Mother, who is shocked by her own rage.

'I don't play cards with madmen.'

'Of course you don't, and *you're* totally normal,' says Mother, 'but you're driving me stark raving mad.'

'D'you hear that?' Mr Java says to the boy. 'Your Mother is suffering from me . . . A clear case of spouso-mania.' He laughs at his own joke and nudges the boy. 'Write it down, nice word.'

Walking to the exit, the boy repeats the strange word a few times under his breath. In the glass hall, where residents and visitors say their goodbyes, he quickly jots it down in his exercise book. Mr Java has to check the spelling. But Mother has already pulled the boy outside. He holds his exercise book up to the glass. Lips read the word. '*OU*,' Mr Java gestures. His corrections don't make it through the glass . . . He uses spit to write on the window.

The boy writes the word in his exercise book with big loops. On purpose. He wants to drag Mr Java home with his lasso.

absence

The sounds at home have changed. No slamming doors, no furious steps in the hall or shards that take away your appetite. The forbidding voice, the creeping eye tiptoeing around – the boy doesn't hear them any more. He can do what he likes, but now it's allowed (lying on the bed with shoes on, eating in the street), it's no fun. Mother and the girls don't agree, they're having the time of their lives: playing forbidden records, tuning the radio to a cheerful station, Mother has stopped putting up her hair, she's even wearing slacks (they make a different sound as well) – not trousers for gardening or storm, but slacks for the whole day. Mr Java would be up on his hind legs if he saw her like that. Next thing she'll be smoking in the street! And every day there's more junk. The magazine rack is overflowing, the bureau is a mess, no one picks off the dried-out geranium leaves. Mr Java's absence is piling up.

The boy sweeps clean, he vacuums, straightens the bikes in the hall, lays a clean newspaper under the leaking moped, uses Vim to clean the scratches the black handgrips have left on the whitewash and, once everything is tidied up – clean, ordered and in piles, the way Mr Java likes it – he gets the polisher out of the cupboard and drags it over to the dull lino. As soon as the motor is turning, the brushes start dragging *him* around, from left to right, between chairs, table and sideboard, banging against the legs – he polishes the house until it's a house of mirrors, making it whole and gleaming again. He admires himself in the lake of beeswax . . . he's never seen himself so handsome and brown before, and tall, he seems to have grown . . . And then he jumps, turning around with a jerk, looking for the shadow he expects to find behind him, the menacing shadow that always makes him so small, the shadow of Mr Java . . . But of course it's not there, the shoes that walk the lino so angrily at home are shuffling around Rosehill.

He works the polisher back and forth across the room, *row-still*, *row-still*, *row-still* . . . The motor sings the name, the brush hums the name, the boy rubs the letters into the lino.

boundless

'I started a letter yesterday, but decided not to send it. You would have grumbled if you'd read it by yourself, because there's something I have to tell you,' Mr Java tells Mother. He stands up for the occasion, buttons his jacket, pulls the letter out of his inside pocket. He's going to declaim it like a poem:

My love is no beauty, but I can't get through a night without her.

She creaks, she buzzes, she's difficult, she's lost her shine.

Her linen breast has grown ragged.

She has a winking bright-green eye and a glowing heart: six valves.

When she weeps (especially at night) she's lost for words and I must help her in her search.

The smallest little thing disturbs her.

But that sensitivity is what lets you hear so much. All the languages of the world. The rustling universe.

Oh, how I love my radio.

Her songs especially cheer me up. I couldn't care less whether I understand the words, the tune is irrelevant.

Take the French, they sing the whole day long. You know them, surely? They sing of love in everything:

In villages in cities in women in cannons in horses.

In Indochina. In the whole universe.

Their love knows no bounds.

But how far can you go?

I believe in faithfulness. In the husband who follows his wife overseas. In the wife who doesn't leave her husband. Not like my mother, who got through five husbands and countless lovers. Boundless as well.

I listen to foreign countries to get to know my limits. Doctor's orders. The psychiatrist teaches me modesty, not getting too big for my boots, but living a balanced life with both feet on the ground.

And what about the Italians? The inventors of speech on the radio, they try to explore the heavens with their voices: Mary for intercessions, Peter for reservations. I sing along with Marconi's quartermasters. Volare!

Turn the knob yourself. Careful. Keep a grip, you'll go too far before you know it. A thousand miles on the map is the tiniest turn of the dial. Stop. What you're hearing now is the Voice of America. We know that. Bulldozer amongst the stations, brooks no interference. Speaking of limits: on cloudy days it pushes the Russians out of the air.

Everyone is equal, so say the communists – in joy and sorrow.

So on to medium wave . . . Careful, you almost slide past: Radio Moscow, let's have it! спчшдй *. . . Listen.*

Yes, I've learnt the odd phrase. You never know when it might come in handy. Shall I translate for you?

'Yesterday in the city of Sverdlovsk the two hundred and fifty millionth standardised sausage rolled off the production line to the loud cheers of psychiatrists and workers.'

Is that the same sausage they eat in Siberian penal colonies?

Do the job on the knob! Let unison go. Brno, Budapest, Tallinn, Beromünster. It's all one song.

Go wild with the dial! Hey, d'you hear that, everywhere those same, serious voices reading The News. Even the news knows its place! The world doesn't sing on the hour. At the chiming of the clock, all countries and all stations take stock: conferences, petitions, sections, protests, ultimatums, blown-up bridges, castles in the air, the dead on the front – all things considered, it turns out to be five minutes to midnight on the hour every hour. What symmetry.

Go on, give it another twist and find out what you've missed!

Mr Java operates his radio like a professional. Marseilles, Kalundborg, Naples, Hilversum, Murmansk . . . His nostrils shiver with excitement. 'Got it! D'you know her? Yma Sumac ... An Inca princess, a sun worshipper. Listen to that stratospheric power. Five octaves out of a single throat, what a range, what pride: "*Um bah barrrm ooooh iiih fuuuur gheh, gheh hyem eeayyyy boooouah bah!*"' Mr Java sings along.

'Can you understand that?' Mother asks.

'She sings what I feel.'

'A serious case of radiomania,' says Mother.

behind the curtain 4

'Are you coming for once?' asks Mother.

'Does he ask for us?'

'He's too preoccupied with himself to be interested in anyone else.'

'Then he doesn't miss us either.'

'He tried to be a father to you.'

'You're talking in the past tense . . . Have you already given him up for dead?'

'You're cruel.'

'What about you? You walk around the house singing. Do *you* miss him?'

'Sometimes, at night . . . the bed's so empty and cold.'

'Turn up the electric blanket.'

a head full of letters

Life was always snapping at his heels, said Mr Java
. . . he was always nervous and there were always
letters, letters from the dear sirs, answers that
demanded answers that were answered with a letter,
letters that demanded letters, and there was always
something on the mat, and what was on the mat was
on his heart, yes, his heart was heavy and his head
was light and then he couldn't sleep, and walked
around at night, light on, light off, bed in, bed out,
radio on, radio off, and then he got to thinking, he
thought up the best letters, and then he wrote an
answer to the letter that still had to come. He already
had four letters on their way in response to answers
that hadn't yet arrived, do you understand? And then
there were his calculations as well. Sums. Sheets full
of numbers. No end of them. Do you understand?
The boy looks at his father. He understands.

bomb dance

'And, are you conversing yet?' Mother asks as she and the boy step into the conversation room at Rosehill.

'I wouldn't dream of it, I have more than enough to tell myself,' says Mr Java.

Mother can't resist a mocking glance, but she doesn't rise to the bait: she has an appointment to see the medical superintendent about the new medication. Anyone can see that the sleeping hasn't helped. Composure is called for. 'So what do you say to yourself?'

'I only come here to pace . . . I need room to think.' Mr Java's words are so loud and agitated that the other patients immediately jump up out of their Danish chairs. Mother gestures for them to stay sitting, but he doesn't even notice them. 'There's nothing wrong with me in here,' Mr Java raps hard on his gleaming skull . . . *tap, tap.* The boy looks up with a start . . . it sounds so hollow. 'You have to chastise your brains,' Mr Java explains, 'brain gymnastics, daily, without fail. The more you use your brain, the fitter it gets. If you don't do anything and sit around all day playing cards like the loonies here, it dries out and shrivels up like a mushroom inside your head.' Another crazy, hard rap.

The patients slink out of the room.

'I've done quite a few calculations walking back and forth and it's time to apply the results.' His smile is weirder than ever. 'Don't you have to go see the superintendent?' he asks Mother.

Calm down . . . she's on her way.

Mr Java takes his pupil into his confidence. 'Pay attention, this is for your ears only: after meticulous study I know that I can do it. Most of the calculations have already been done by others, I just adopt their results, there's no need for us to re-invent complexities . . . I don't discover, I apply! The detonation is a question of counting, endless series of numbers . . . but I've got there! There's only one problem left: what do we do with the neutrons that are released? Two or three are released with each atom we split. On average! How do we absorb that?' Another blow to his skull – as if he's knocking on a wooden box – and then the boy sees it: when Mr Java raps on his head with one hand, he hits something hard behind his back with the other. He tugs at his trousers and pulls a big, hard book out from under the back of his tweed jacket, stuck in under his belt, concealed in the hollow between buttocks and back, Mr Java's favourite storage place – you keep your hands free and no one can see what you're carrying. When he opens it the cover clacks on the Danish table. There are rows of numbers in it, neat digits in blue squares, page after page. He shows his calculations – briefly. 'It's the application that matters, leave the comprehension to me.' He slams the book shut. 'Bomb Book' it says on the label.

Mr Java has not just been doing his sums, he has also put his hands to work. There was nothing else for it, he had to do something during the compulsory hours of occupational therapy. 'The name alone is a punishment,' he says. 'Erase it, forget! They taught me how to gouge,' he scowls. 'Scratching trees in a piece of lino with a blunt chisel. Trees with roots. Long roots, deep emotions. I thought, What do I want with a tree? Gouge a bomb.' Mr Java whistles in the boy's ear. '*Tally-ho, big bomb show* . . .' It makes his earwax buzz. 'Now that's a therapy,' says Mr Java.

The third bomb. 'Someone has to make it. Someone has to preserve the balance.'

But we're not there yet, there are still a few niggling little problems. Mr Java leafs through his calculations. 'The radius of action . . .' He counts, the numbers rattle through his brain. 'The smaller, the better.'

The boy gives himself over to his role as pupil. 'A small one, not a big one,' he repeats, 'the smaller, the better.'

Mr Java gives a satisfied nod. 'You know, an atomic bomb needs a powerful reflector, armour casing that slows down the explosion. Extremely important. In our case it has to be very strong armour. If we get that, it's ready.'

Someone knocks on the door. After some loud throat-clearing the knocking stops. 'This room is for thinking, not playing cards!' Mr Java roars at the keyhole. Putting his words into action, he starts walking in circles . . . on the coconut mat, around the coconut mat . . . reducing and increasing his radius of action . . . and after umpteen circles he gets dizzy and bangs his shin on a Danish chair, 'Rrraaaaasssssssmussen!'

Mr Java racks his brains: current hydrogen bombs are too powerful and too big. With transportation difficulties: whale sized. His will be portable: six pounds and not an ounce more. And the radius of action will be no larger than the coconut mat. Ten, maybe twelve feet? Difficult calculations, he kneads and raps his skull. 'It's just a question of the inside,' he says, 'I've finished the outside.'

Two disbelieving eyes look at him.

'Want to see it?'

The boy jumps up.

Mr Java slams the bomb book shut and leaves the room.

—

The boy lays his hands on the bomb book to stop the sums from getting away. His hands are sticky, the numbers in the bomb book are glowing. No, his hand doesn't open it, not even a chink, no matter how much the book wants him to. He strokes the marbled edge: red, orange, blue and yellow waves – the sky after an atom bomb. He's seen the colour photos in *Life*. A scorched sky over a trembling sea . . . red, orange, azure . . . under it lay Eniwetok, the atoll that had been wiped off the face of the earth in a single blow. First hydrogen bomb test. Eniwetok . . . it sounds like an Indian word, a smoke signal the whole world could understand. Mr Java has shown him the photo more than once – a trembling sea in trembling hands. And now those same hands have made a hydrogen bomb.

Here comes the bomb knocking on the door. It sails into the room, steered by Mr Java's hand. As promised: small. Mackerel sized. He dances around with it. Spinning on the coconut mat, circling the magazine rack. Oh, if the Russians could see this! The bliss on Mr Java's face!

'Feel it, take it . . . it's so light.'

It's a brown bomb cut out of a piece of linoleum. Mr Java sails up to the boy. Roaring with laughter. The boy presses himself hard against the wall. What's got into him? Come on, join the dance! Doesn't he understand? Mr Java is doing it all for him, there's nothing to be scared of. It's a bomb that knows its limitations, just a little circle, no bigger than the coconut mat, even if it has the power of a thousand suns. Mr Java strokes his bomb. He presses his cheek against a thousand suns. All love, through and through.

the next Sunday

They all dropped by: ministers, members of parliament, party bigwigs, leading civil servants, arms dealers, a handful of professors, a news-reader or two, four-star generals, politicians, heads of state. Monkey was invited and so were Mikoyan and Khrushchev. Along with a bunch of fellow travellers and armchair communists, but of course none of them showed up, the cowards. But those who did were burning with curiosity. Anyway, the whole troop was shown into the conversation room. Apologies all round for it being such a crush, so many big shots on one coconut mat. Lights out and the demonstration could begin. They passed the bomb around in the dark – no details, national secret, they could understand that – and weighed it in their hands, discussing pluses and minuses in all the world's languages. Everyone wanted to hold it for a moment, the handy H-bomb. The capitalists wanted to buy it blind. The socialists all wanted to get their paws on it at the same time, so none of them managed. And then he locked the door. The windows were bolted. 'Stay calm, please, gentlemen,' Mr Java shouted, 'have faith in progress!'

—

The explosion was simply stunning. The deafening bang followed by a magnificent mushroom. Mr Java rapped on his skull contentedly – a modest noise this time. With relish he described the lovely fresh breeze the day after the explosion. Virtually no fallout. Besides the mess the politicians left behind – that was disgusting. But otherwise the world was much cleaner afterwards.

Shame about all those important people.

Mr Java whistles a tune and adopts a jaunty expression. The tune takes on words. '*Pour fabriquer une bombe "A", mes enfants croyez-moi, c'est vraiment de la tarte* . . . Ha-ha-ha.' Heard time and again on his song radio. Ha-ha-ha, Mr Java came through without a scratch. The Danish table came in handy after all . . . Duck and take cover – no one needs to tell the leading light of the Civil Defence Corps what to do. He's bombproof.

And now the occupational therapist wants to know the ins and outs of it all. 'Of course, I just act like I'm crazy.'

assassination

The mirror pilot has a proposition: Why don't we do it together? My P-38 is at your disposal.

It will be a long flight, but I know the way. Money's no problem. Plenty of supplies. The only question is: how? Fly in high, above the cloud cover, dive down and blast away with all we've got? Wrong tactic: Monkey has an air-raid shelter. Somehow you have to get into his house . . . A nylon thread at the top of the stairs, that's stood the test of time, that's how they get each other to take a fall in the Kremlin. Monkey is sure to have an impressive staircase, the kind of ceremonial staircase dictators have in the news-paper. An invisible thread, strung an inch over the top step . . . Monkey tries to walk down and goes head over heels . . . broken neck. A pistol against the temple is another option, but difficult. Bullets are noisy and how do you get away after the shot? Palace guards grab you by the scruff of the neck and you hang. No, it has to be done quietly, only one person has to die and he's it. A knife is a favourite weapon in those parts. Muddy your face and lie in wait behind the bamboo until he comes by – jump up and stab him in the neck. Twist the blade to sever an artery and he's dead.

The boy practises on sand. Not the loose stuff, but the hard wet layer underneath. He scrapes an area clean and uses the point of his pocket knife to draw the outline of a shadow. Now aim for the neck, with a steady hand, get it in the middle first go . . . His vibrating knife thuds into the great thief's throat. Sand flies up. Necked!

Monkey's sticky blood in the notch of his blade: that is the proof he will bring back. Saviour of the father-land. In the carriage next to the queen.

The boy lies on his back in the dunes, in the spring sun, with the mirror pilot's exercise book on his stomach. Something has to happen. But nobody does anything! If Mr Java wasn't so weak, he'd do it. Monkey is back in the news, grinning in the paper every day, and Mr Java is getting madder and madder. Action! Monkey must die . . .

The boy scrapes the sand with his knife, scraping the grin off that ugly mug. The grin of a polygamist . . . 'What will happen to Sukarno if he comes? Yes, what will happen to Sukarno if he comes? We will hack him into pieces, yes, we'll hack him into pieces. We will do that to Sukarno if he comes . . .' That's what they sing at school, but he, Mr Java's pupil, will do more than just sing, he'll do it! And Sukarno won't come here, he'll go there, with the mirror pilot! Again he stabs his knife deep into the sand, his fist glows, the sand burns, cutting into his flesh. He bites and spits on Sukarno the Monkey.

Weary with hatred he slumps down on the dead dictator. He could think him dead, or pray him dead. If he concentrated, he could send out lightning bolts, atom rays, through the skies and into Sukarno's skull, right through that black flowerpot. Bombs fly out of his head, bombs to blow up *Bung Karno*.

Or shall they scorch his palace with a magnifying glass? There's a bottle of rat poison left in the stables, and the axe; he's never scared when he's got the axe . . . and so he falls asleep with clenched fists. Hero to the nation. Hero to Mr Java.

dream

Mother and the girls call for help, they are sick and lying in the bomb shelter. The boy keeps watch at the hatch. He opens a tin of hardtack (use before the end of World War III), fills the kettle from the water bottles – the tap water is contaminated – and turns up the meths burner. The pot of salted beans is empty, there is mould in the preserving jars. Tea and hardtack are the only things they can keep down. A deathly pale first sister holds out her cup, she's losing blood, her nightie is red. She vomits on the bedspread. Mother and the other two girls are delirious on their pallets. They're feverish, with headaches. Shivering. The boy takes a dishcloth and cleans up the mess. Outside it's daytime and dark, warm rain seeps through the cellar walls. Nature is confused. Mr Java knocks on the hatch, he's been to the village for final instructions. Blood is trickling out of his ears. All contacts have been broken. The rubber tyres of the Civil Defence Corps jeep have melted. Mr Java kneels before first sister, wipes her face clean with his linen handkerchief and kisses her. They hug. Outside the horses are drumming.

the stone

Mr Java sits at the window, enjoying the sun through the glass. He fidgets with a stone he found in the Rosehill garden, a pebble from a river. The boy is standing behind him. 'What a journey a stone like this has made,' says Mr Java. He tosses it up, rubs it warm, weighs it in the palm of his hand.

The boy impresses the image on his memory: Mr Java in pyjamas, playing with a pebble . . . in green spring light, on a plain wooden chair . . . looking skinny and frail. A small, strange man. For the first time in his life the boy is not scared of him.

'Son, you know what I feel like doing?' asks Mr Java without looking at him, tossing up the stone. 'What I have an irresistible urge to do?'

'No.'

'Throw this stone right in your face.' Mr Java laughs.

The boy is scared again.

an unexpectedly warm day

'An elephant is trumpeting in my head,' Mr Java tells
the boy. 'D'you hear it, smash, crack, do you smell it?
An elephant. God, it stinks. We had two, in the old
days. For dragging tree trunks or clearing land after
a storm or a tropical downpour. The heavy work.
They tidied up, but they were messy too. When they
dropped a turd, you heard the thunder for miles
around. Turds as big as tea cosies. But sacred . . . You
didn't dare touch them, the turds were for the keepers.
Each elephant had its own keeper. And each keeper
had his turds. They fed the animal, went to the river
with it, washed it, cleaned its teeth and . . . they
watched over its turds. Each turd got its own little
flag. Because brewing in each turd was a delicacy that
was worth a pretty penny at the market: dung beetles.
Just let it bake in the sun and wait for them to fatten
themselves up and crawl out contentedly. Then impale
them on the spot and roast them over a bamboo fire.
Until they burst out of their jackets. Sometimes,
when the harvest was especially rich, there was a
beetle left over for us. It was a delicacy we children
would fight over. Ah . . . what a taste, when I think

back on it . . . On glorious, unexpectedly warm days like today I hear them scratching under my skull. Beetles yearning for the sun and looking for a way out of their dung heap.' Mr Java almost licks his lips at the thought . . .

'*Kerchunk, kerchunk,*' he says and jumps on the locomotive of his memories.

The boy doesn't ride with him, he stays behind, at a loss for words.

Mother says there weren't any elephants on Java.

the swimmer

'So, managed after all?' asks an unshaven Mr Java as he opens the door of his room. 'An hour late! Have I been cancelled? Are you already getting used to me not existing? Some people have been here five years and they get visitors every Sunday, yes.' The foam flies from his lips. Even the tea trolley passed him by. 'And Sundays are already so much emptier than weekdays.' Angrily he turns his back on his visitors. 'Keep your coats on, the bell will ring any minute now and you'll have to go again.'

Middle sister and third sister put a heavy basket down on his bed. Yes, they've come along . . . for the first time in months and look how happy Mr Java is.

'You can take that basket back with you.' He refuses to even look at it.

'Fruit cake, apple pie!' The girls push two baking trays under his nose.

'There's nothing to celebrate here.'

'Then we'll eat them up,' says Mother, panting as she takes off her coat, 'we just spent two flaming hours on the stinking local, there were cows on the track.'

And where is first sister?

Too busy. Finals. She's very sorry.

Mother lays the post on his lap. Mr Java lets the letters slip down between his legs. 'Feeble excuses.' He doesn't offer any chairs, nothing. Mother and the two girls sit down bored on the bed, coats behind them. The boy takes his book and stares blankly at the next page.

Mr Java sulks. Mother's very sorry for him, she says, that it took so long. She feels guilty, but what can she do about it?

'Nothing,' grumbles Mr Java, 'not a thing.'

The sun shines through the narrow window. Shadow leaves sway on the wall. The visitors look round and eat cake, slice after slice, knocking off the apple pie as well – if you eat you don't need to talk. Disagreeing isn't safe.

'Where's the radio?' asks Mother eventually.

'Removed. Superintendent's orders. It's a mystery how he knew about it . . .' Mother studies the ceiling. 'The walls have ears,' says Mr Java, 'but now I've got something they won't hear coming: shadow TV.'

What? Where?

'There!' He points at the spot where the sunlight meets the wallpaper. 'My fair-weather station. Good and cheap.' A cruel smile plays on his lips. Mr Java moves his chair and sits down with his back to the bed. They're welcome to watch over his shoulder. He uses his sleeve to wipe the dust out of the sun. Clear picture. 'Today: Jungleman! *Ta-ta-ta-taaaa!*' Mr Java announces himself. Invisible mosquitoes swarm out of the wall. He swats two dead. Mother pulls the ribbon around her bun tighter and checks her watch. The two girls nudge each other.

Minutes pass.

Something really is growing in the muggy room. The boy sees it too. Not on the wall that Mr Java has papered with his fantasies. No, it's growing in Mr Java himself . . . in his face. The folds around his eyes disappear, his chin gets tighter, his face becomes as smooth and shiny as a television tube, as the tablets in the bottle on his bedside cabinet. Another Mr Java is sitting on the chair, as if he's traded himself in for a younger man.

'See how you need to hack your way down a jungle path,' he says, 'every trek it's the same.' His finger follows the patches of sun – mountain paths. 'But we weren't the first, many had gone before us.' And there, behind that shadow, he walks . . . His cutlass in his right hand, strap around his wrist, carbine over his left shoulder. Blade and senses sharp . . . Forward march! In before sunset.

Mr Java's headpower travelling is nothing new to the boy. Before being admitted to Rosehill he would often set off, standing at the window with his hands in his pockets, looking at things you couldn't see outside. At first the boy had been jealous, and scared that Mr Java would never turn round again, that he would stay standing there stiffly in front of the window, with his back to the sitting room, gone for ever to an inner world where he met mysterious people. He seemed to go further and further . . . But he always came back, calmer and usually cheerful. The boy has learnt to join him in his travels, he doesn't even need to look at the warm wall. He too sees the film that goes with the story Mr Java is telling . . . Soldiers wading across a river, up the bank and into the mountains, headed for a remote outstation, three days' march. The sun glitters on his skull. It is a difficult journey for him and his men, but more difficult still for the prisoners they have to deliver.

'Communists . . .'

'Rebels,' corrects Mother, who has been drawn in against her wishes. The girls pull faces and make a show of covering their ears with their hands.

'They're dying of thirst,' says Mr Java, 'they beg for water, collapsing with exhaustion, holding each other tight, legs chained together. The path is narrow: if

259

one falls, he'll drag the rest with him.' Mr Java looks down from his chair.

The boy estimates the depth of the chasm . . .

Mr Java pulls up his legs. 'One's slipping now,' he shouts, 'on a loose stone, he grabs . . . no, too wet, too slippery, there they go, one by one. They're falling, they're falling!'

The girls can no longer keep up their feigned deafness. Third sister shakes the tablet bottle. 'Very funny,' says middle sister coolly. 'The superintendent said this would stop.'

Mother forces Mr Java to look the other way, away from the shadow TV. She tugs at his chair. But he pushes her aside – out of his picture – he grabs at chains slipping through his fingers. 'You're raving,' she says, her bun bobbing. The girls come over and stand in front of him. 'Relax, relax . . . take a deep breath.' But he tears himself free of the skirts . . . he hacks his way free and falls on the bed. He rips the blankets aside, clawing at the sheets with his hands, burying his head under the coats. The girls try to calm him, they grab him by his jacket, his trouser legs . . . Mr Java kicks them away . . . They look at the red marks on their arms, helpless . . . Sniffing, they run out into the corridor to get a doctor.

'Yuck,' says Mother, shocked by the colour of the mattress and sheets, 'they don't change the bedclothes.'

Mr Java is swimming under the coats and sheets. A smell of dirty socks splashes up.

The boy hides behind his book . . . it's the first time he's seen Mr Java change into a fish. He's used to transformations: shuddering shoulders, trembling ears, whinnying – little things, twitches – but now there really is a fish with tweed scales swimming there. Nimble and free. The bed has become a river, the water rustles in the sheets.

Mother gives up and sits down, she doesn't know what else to do. 'He's living my nightmare,' she says. '*I* saw prisoners falling into a ravine, *I* walked through the mountains with soldiers, hacking a path in the gloom, following the cutlass and . . . I told him about it so many times . . . *Him? Pfhhh* . . . he doesn't even dare to hold a knife. He steals my stories.' Pityingly she watches him thrash away.

Mr Java eats his way through the mattress cover. The kapok boils out. Now he's swimming in rapids. White waves churn over the sides. The sun is gone.

Slide the chair back a little . . . Keep dry. 'I think it's time for another injection,' Mother says with one eye on the door. 'Go and see what's keeping the girls and the doctor.'

silent album

The boy gets Mr Java's photo album out of the bookcase and takes it into his bedroom. And there, on the
bed, he cracks the glued spine to his heart's content,
he rustles the cobweb paper between the photos, he
runs his fingers through the jungle. But the old East
Indies won't start moving, not without Mr Java's
detailed explanations . . . the outrigger proa is stuck
in the mud, the rubber congeals, the Hispano–Suiza
seizes up.

His index finger strokes the women: the tennis players,
the rally drivers, the equestrians, the hikers in tall
grass, the dancers under palm trees. The women who
dragged Mr Java through it all. What's keeping them
this time? They smile. They don't stretch out a single
hand. Not even when he pinches them . . . tears their
skirts, rips the horses to pieces, pulls away the tennis
net and shreds the sepia gardens. Not a peep out of
them when the boy takes the remnants of their lives
to the dunes and sets fire to them. Flames lick around
the verandas. Evening gowns scorch and disappear.
Hillsides of coffee and tea catch alight. Krakatoa curls

up. A steamboat smokes a big cigar. The equator evaporates . . .

Tropical heat.

The mirror pilot whispers, 'Stick your finger in the flame, then you're a man.'

The boy does it. For a second.

Then he pisses on the ash. A dark river flows through the sand.

rice

'I have such a longing for bright colours,' Mr Java says dully, 'please, wear something else next time, I'm suffering visual deprivation.' He stares disapprovingly at Mother's grey suit, robust and not crumpled at all, not even after a tiring journey. 'Everything in this building is grey and cream – the walls, the ceilings, the corridors – if I stay here much longer, they'll paint my insides grey-cream as well.' He vomits it out, 'Grey-cream! They even boil the food down into grey-cream snot. I have to get out of here as soon as I can.'

'Stick it out just a little longer, finish the new course of therapy. Then life will take on colour again by itself.'

Mr Java raps on his skull (the old gesture). 'I'm going to trade myself in.' He glares at the bottles, jars and powders next to his bed. 'No more headpower,' he tells the boy.

Mother pulls a pan of fried rice out of her bag to supplement the Rosehill snot. '*Nasi goreng* . . .' sighs Mr Java, at least that's got taste and colour.

Ah, how much tastier rice was there than it is here . . . There, where the rice grows green in the water. There, where the chaff floats through the air after drying and winnowing. The mountain of rice in the courtyard . . . filling the sacks, then sticking your hand in and feeling the grains under your nails . . . Mother and Mr Java daydream together on their hardwood chairs. The boy slouches on the bed and sees their eyes glow, they look up, feel the sun. Mr Java describes the clicking of dry rice in a pan — the only rain he likes the sound of.

And the sky . . . 'The sky was bluer there, wherever you looked.'

'And higher, you don't get big puffy clouds like that here.'

'Sometimes they weren't even clouds, they were flocks of ibises . . .'

'You never forget that smell.'

'See, you can still enjoy things,' says Mother.

Mr Java lights a cigarette, they draw on it in turns and blow out clouds of their own . . . Mother blushes from the memories and the shared happiness, but Mr Java turns even paler, becoming parchment, yellowish white like the faces in the burnt family album. 'Someone else has . . .'

'Don't think about it, you're alive.'

'From just twelve feet.'

'You're indestructable.'

'I used to be, yes.'

'Think of the things you'll be able to do again soon.'

Mr Java doesn't answer.

'There must be something you long for.'

'Servants,' says Mr Java dully, 'lots of staff.'

'You've got that here already,' says Mother. 'No, something you can long for at home.'

Mr Java rests and hammers his head . . . what, yes, what? 'Vacuuming my pockets.' That's something he longs for. He misses the lovely sound of the nozzle swallowing the lining of an inside pocket: *plopfurlfff-plepf.*

'You could do a course,' Mother prompts.

And arranging all the letters in piles . . . yes, that's something else he'd like – he hardly notices Mother's suggestions. 'In and out piles for the post. And doing the house with Vim. Touching up all the scratches. Fixing the toilet. Soaking the girls' combs in ammonia . . .' And soaking his nails in the bath and then trimming them. Ten crescent moons – none broken. That's something he hasn't managed at Rosehill, where he is only allowed to shower for three minutes once a week. Cutting nice moons, that's something he longs

266

for. And wallpapering the dinette. He screws up his eyes and wishes as hard as he can: Mr Java materialises a brand-new home.

But most of all he'd like to stretch out in the heat under a dark-green leafy tree – a roof the sun slips through – and wait for the cool breeze of evening.

'Yes, the gardens,' Mother says and tries again. 'You could take up gardening, rose-growing.'

Tea roses. A beautiful yellow. The room is sparkling with desire. Memories shoot back and forth, faster than the speed of light. And then the demons come back. 'Beautiful, yellow dusters, they're lovely too, and the dustpan, ah, I wonder how my dustpan is.'

Mr Java is happy. Mother looks for a hanky for her tears.

The boy hurls the pan of golden fried rice out of the window.

a full suitcase

Which clothes is the boy taking? His red blouse. *Blouse?* Mother stares at him as if a stranger has appeared before her. 'Do you say blouse? Boys wear shirts.'

Knickers? 'Say, underpants.'

Shorts? 'Take a pair of long trousers too, there are lots of flies there. No, don't call them slacks. Trousers.'

'What about your good jacket?' Too Sundayish for a farm. 'Their Sundays are more Sunday than our Sundays.'

A top? 'What's got into you? That's a pullover!'

He talks like a girl. Soon, when he's with real boys, he'll have to watch his words. The baby words too. His PJs become pyjamas, his wellies boots, and his willy? '*Dick*,' that's what the labourers say in the rag-and-bone paddock. Dick it is. The boy is growing up.

His Sunday trousers are too short, he can't show up there with them at half mast like that. To assure herself that it really is him inside his body, Mother measures him up with the tape measure and immediately sits down at the pedal sewing-machine to make a new pair of long trousers from one of her old skirts. A red–and–blue kilt is the only one she can get his length out of.

Mother is rough on the fabric, she's in a hurry. She knows she has made a harsh decision, but it can't go on like this. The situation is untenable. The things the boy has got up to these last few weeks! He is out of control . . . that pan of rice . . . and he steals, he cheats, he bunks off school and shows an unhealthy curiosity. Yes, he has broken open the secret drawers of Mr Java's bureau, jumbled up the documents, gone at the stock box with a hammer and, as if that's not bad enough, he hacked his globe lampshade (where Mr Java's shadow hangs over the equator) in half with the axe – a birthday present, of all things! And why? He doesn't know why. He was looking for something for school. He was bored.

What the boy needs is a firm hand. Strong men he can take as an example. Mother spoke to the school, then called her family. 'Put him on the train,' was the answer from the clay country. Leave it to them, they'll turn him into a healthy boy.

And now the suitcase is on his bed with its jaws open. Stuffed with men's clothing, the schoolwork has already been packed, the mirror pilot is hidden under his new tartan trousers. Mother tidies and irons and, when she's looking the other way, twenty guilders from her housekeeping purse decide to make the trip with the boy. It's not stealing, it's for emergencies, in case he has to buy his freedom in unknown territory.

Something else that has to go with him is a long list of good advice.

– Don't suck your tongue. 'It makes you pout, boys don't pout,' says Mother.

– No skipping. 'If you're in a hurry, run.'

– Don't let your nose do the talking. 'When you see horse droppings on the street, think, Hey, what a lovely clump of grass!'

– Stop scratching and picking. 'It makes other people nervous.'

– Ignore mirrors. 'Looking at yourself all the time won't make you any prettier.'

– Don't pull faces. 'We're not on the stage here.'

– Know your place. 'You're at your best when no one notices you.'

The girls stand by grinning and nodding.

Mother hangs a label around his neck with instructions for the conductor, she's got too much to worry about to take the boy to her family herself: that's why she's sending him as a living package. Yes, it will be a journey full of dangers: he is the first one in the family to go to stay on the farm. 'And if you ruin it,' say the girls, 'you'll ruin our inheritance as well.'

The suitcase isn't big enough for so much good advice.

on the farm

There's still a crust of sea salt on the outside walls, a white waist-high line, but otherwise there's not a thing left from the whole flood – after four years Mother's family have their heads well above water. And there's plenty of it in and around the farmhouse: puddles, mud pools and greasy drops on the grass. They throw buckets of suds over the kitchen floor, they couldn't care less about wetting the table legs. They're hearty scrubbers, the boy could learn a thing or two from that, but they can't flush the stench out of his nose. He sneezes from early in the morning until late at night. Whenever an aunt, uncle or cousin gets too close, he splutters them away again. It's the manure, cow and pig atoms in the air, he says. No, it's not that he thinks the farm's dirty – really, he doesn't – he can see for himself how clean they keep their clothes. Every day they flutter on the washing line: blue overalls with three-foot flies, cow-sized underpants, bras you could row away in, nightshirts and big pods flapping in the wind – dress shields the women sew under their armpits to soak up the sweat of the day. The boy has already nicked one of them and now he wants his jacket back. His pilot's collar races through the corn here, his cousin Bartholomew considers it his property. They've got their eyes on his tartan trousers as well, Aunt Marie thinks they're much too citified and made him take them off the moment he arrived. She gave him overalls in exchange – at half mast.

Once the day's work is done, neighbours and fellow villagers come and go – everyone's related, which means they're related to him as well. They all look the same: short legs, black hair. A reminder of the Eighty Years' War, so they say: the Spaniards wreaked havoc in West Brabant and the villagers have been stunted ever since. That's how long it takes for a war to blow over, but no one makes *them* clear their plates if they don't want to. Leftovers go to the pigs.

Their names haven't progressed since the days the Spanish ruled the roost either. Half the village shares a single surname and those who do choose from five Christian names, it's been like that for centuries. You can hardly tell the family apart! It's Leonard with the goat or Leonard with the ears, and Marie from behind the church, who lives next door to boatyard Marie's Adrian, who's a second cousin of Bartholomew from the heath's Marie . . . The boy gets lost in his relations. 'And you's one of us too, ain't yer?'

'We're from the Indies,' he says.

'Don't be daft.' They annex him. Whether he likes it or not: he's named after them.

He even has to share a bed with them. Every night he and his cousin Bartholomew thump each other left and right, and every morning they wake up in the middle. Bartholomew is covered with calluses, he's older and stronger, but he doesn't have a writer's lump. The hardest thing about him is the stiffy he wakes up with every morning.

After lots of nagging he lets the boy have a good look at it: it throbs, it's red with blue veins and it stinks. There's a glistening drop on the end. 'Cripes,' the boy says.

'Cursing's not allowed,' says Bartholomew.

The Spaniards might have kept Mother's family small, but there's no shortage in the dick department. You should see black Len's! Every day he puts on a show in the barn. In two shakes he spatters white globs in the hay. Good for the mice, he says.

He uses those same hands to say grace at dinner, thanking God for the lavish abundance. Uncle Leonard (Adrian's Aunt Marie's) and Aunt Marie (first cousin to Leonard with the ears) nod encouragingly. The things they serve are 'nourishment for our sinful hearts'. They're even fussier about it than Aunt Mina (a cousin to Aunt Marie from behind the church, who's from the same branch as Leonard with the ears). It's all thank you, Lord this and thank you, Lord that.

During prayer the boy studies his relatives more closely: their weather-beaten necks and hunched shoulders, and the lines in their faces. Faces that are tuned to crass sounds: iron scraping over cement, the squeak of pumps, udders pissing into empty buckets, stamping clogs, mooing, bleating and cackling – sounds that get under your skin.

When they eat he hears the milk frothing in their mugs and the pig's trotters dancing in the soup. Even headpower doesn't help him to get down the greasy beans, but Aunt Marie doesn't notice: his cousins swipe anything he doesn't like off his plate and Uncle Leonard praises her cooking.

'Are these 'uns from November still?'

'No, those are pickling.'

'What are these then?'

'These came with Hubert's rent.'

'With the spuds?'

'Yes, they're fine spuds, aren't they?'

'They make a fine meal, Marie.'

'If you didn't think they made a fine meal, Leonard, they'd be no good at all.'

'But they do make a good meal.'

And then they all make a meal of it.

—

His cousins put the boy to work helping with the food. Turning apples in the drying loft, weeding the vegetable garden – where he secretly pats the oxheart cabbages, strokes the turnip tops and whispers encouragement to the broad beans, because Uncle Leonard is worried that they won't manage in the brackish soil. Digging the earth, he feels like a real farmer. He would have made a good planter – in the Indies, if it was still theirs. Pricking out the spinach plants, he even pretends he's working in a rice paddy. The pale green leaves seek the south . . . Yes, then it's all right for the drizzle to soak him and he's proud of the dark edges under his nails. But scrubbing the wooden stepladder (the one they tie the pigs to before cutting their throats and letting them bleed to death upside-down) with the same brush they use to de-hair the pigs in boiling water, he vomits over his hands. 'Ah, deary, that's naught to make a fuss about,' says cousin Adrian.

—

Not a day goes by without the boy learning something new. All the things he learns from Scripture! Every evening after dinner they take turns to read out loud . . . more war and misery than Mr Java ever got out of a newspaper. The Lord's camp makes the camps in the tropics look soft. And every man at the table takes it in his stride. Faith makes you tougher – that's lesson number one. And Paradise is not located on the equator, but in the heavens above – lesson number two. And 'the old days' is not a better place, a better place is in the future and you go there when you die – lesson number three. Death is an all-round improvement – that's another lesson that gets thrown unexpectedly in the boy's lap.

The boy is lucky: an Uncle Hubert has died, at ninety-six, after a long sick-bed. He's only a distant relative, even if he lives just round the corner, but with too much land to take lightly. Thank the Lord. After Uncle Hubert has been praised to high heaven in prayer, the whole family sets out for the home of the deceased and the boy gets to go with them, to 'pay respects' on behalf of his mother. 'He's receiving in his coffin,' says Aunt Marie.

The boy skips to the neighbouring farm – this will be his first dead body! Waiting outside are even more relatives. They open their ranks for him, enclose him, take him up in their number: boys he's never seen before, strapping girls who look him over from a distance, uncles and aunts with hard hands . . . Yes, he's one of 'Wild Marie's'. Inside he is introduced to men and women in black: wedding-and-funeral relatives – the best kind of all.

The coffin is in the upstairs room, which is also crowded with people. When the boy sees the lid leaning against the wall, he turns on the spot, but a maid with a plate of currant loaf pushes him back into the room. 'He won't bite, you know,' she says. And holding the plate with her right hand, she leads him to the coffin with her left.

Uncle Hubert is a picture of respectability. 'I cleaned his shoes,' the maid says. 'With Nivea – that gives the best shine and keeps them good for longer, they're going to have a hard time of it under the ground.' The girl smiles at him cheerfully and presents him with her last slice.

With his mouth full, the boy stares at the body . . . Uncle Hubert must have liked currant loaf as well, by the look of his gut, he's very round. In his church suit, with three buttons of the coat done up. Mr Java would never approve, only the middle button is allowed to be done up. He has an envelope in his hand. What could be inside it? 'Money for the crossing,' according to one cousin.

'A letter for St Peter,' another says.

'No, it's a goodbye message from his great-grandson,' says a blue straw hat that's bent over the coffin. A goodbye message . . . that's why the boy has come as well, on behalf of his mother . . . he whispers it softly.

Uncle Hubert is pink, from the powder, but his ears are blue. Very blue, and gristly and yellowish. There are needle punctures on his hands. 'They had to drain off gallons of fluid,' the maid says, and above the throat, near the chin ('a new shirt, a bit of a waste'), the throat is moving. His Adam's apple throbs, he swallows . . . The boy stares and sniffs, and even when he doesn't dare to keep looking, he's still watching, out of the corner of one eye. The straw hat kisses Uncle's bald head, she strokes him and calls him honeykins. 'That's Aunt Jenny, Beet's second wife,' whispers the maid to the back of his neck. 'Thirty years younger, not from here.' Beet? That's right, that's what they tend to call Huberts here in the village. But Jenny doesn't care and calls him loveykins, honeykins.

Uncle Hubert wants to say something back, the words throb in his throat, but he can't get them out, his lips are clamped shut. 'Stuck together,' the maid says. The boy sees a bubble of air between his lips, a bubble that moves. 'PVA.' They used it to stick down his eyelids as well. 'Had to, didn't they? 'Cause he stunk.' If the boy listens carefully, he can hear Uncle Hubert gurgling.

The visitors don't notice a thing, they talk and sit and drink. A tot of advocaat, some sugared brandy. Cheers. Oh, these savoury biscuits are delicious. Home-made, Jenny? Where does she find the time? Beet loved them too, these 'uns, with the shiny almonds on top.

'Do you want one too, honeykins?' Aunt Jenny holds a biscuit in front of his mouth, rubs it over his lips, presses it on the PVA.

The boy takes a step back. Waiting for the bang.

—

In the evening Uncle Leonard and Aunt Marie entertain a stream of fresh relatives who have been to see their dead uncle. 'Death is the best harvest,' says Uncle Leonard. The men talk about the price of Hubert's land, the women about Jenny's straw hat. Cousins walk in and out and help themselves from full bowls, sweet and salted, it keeps coming. Marzipan dipped in chocolate, cake dipped in marzipan, cheese balls – they pig themselves to death. The boy munches away and feels at home. He has never been away from home this long before. His schoolwork is still in the bottom of his suitcase, no one cares. Working with his hands – that will be his future, that and putting his hands together before the Lord. As long as he joins in prayer, he belongs, and at night in bed he often continues his conversation with God the Father. The mirror pilot is off duty.

Later in the evening, when the gin has appeared on the table and the boy is spooning up advocaat with fluffed milk skin, the men talk politics. Bombs and communists don't get a look-in, the word 'pension' isn't mentioned either. It's all about the price of land

and government rules. 'We're losing our freedom!' 'They've got their paws on our land.' The boy is surprised by how calmly the farmers complain – puffing cigars and sipping their drinks. Mr Java would have hit the roof three times, but they say: the laws come from God Almighty. And whatever God ordains is right – they sing that in their hymns and they accept it. According to Uncle Leonard the authorities carry not the sword in vain.

Instead of being a farmer, one uncle is a pen-pusher from the city and works out all kinds of things for the farmers. 'I tell you, you're being robbed. I tell you, the state is a thief.' Cigars and faces glow. Yes, the big-shot minister is a thief.

'We were robbed too,' says the boy, desperate to put his oar in.

'How's that?' asks the city uncle.

'In the Indies.'

'In the Indies? How?' snaps the city uncle.

'The horses, and the houses, the bearer bonds . . . and the hiss . . . the hisspanosweeze,' the boy stammers.

'Whose? Has Wild Marie . . .' The uncles and aunts all cackle at the same time. Has Wild Marie inherited or not, and who from? Isn't Mina looking . . .

'All gone,' says the boy. 'The pepper gardens too.'

'Ha!' mocks the city uncle. 'The colonialists were the biggest robbers, they're telling you stories.'

The farmers growl their agreement, 'Our Adrian's a red, but he tells it like it is.'

'Of course, we mustn't get things mixed up,' sniffs the city uncle. 'Ruining our market with cheap cane sugar, as if our beets are inferior, wood under the price, rice for a pittance . . . and all out of the hides of the poor natives.'

'My father's a native,' the boy says seriously.

The family roars with laughter. 'Yes, he was a dark horse, that father of yours . . . has he got a job yet?' asks the city uncle. The laughter dies down, a circle of eyes look at the boy. 'Or is his lordship still too high and mighty? Pepper gardens, my arse, all lost and gambled away. That mother of his — five husbands, wasn't it? She spent like there was no tomorrow.'

Frightened, the boy looks into his glass of advocaat.

'Does Wild Marie let him fob off all those lies?' the city uncle asks Aunt Marie. 'All those letters she's written complaining about it.'

'It's Sukarno's fault,' the boy says quietly. And then again, out loud, 'Sukarno's a thief.'

'Sukarno doesn't steal, he reinstates.'

282

'He's a monkey.'

Well this, well that, have you ever! The farmers are flabbergasted. 'Who's the cheeky monkey round here?'

'Goddammit,' the boy curses, throwing his advocaat down on the floor.

Uncles, aunts and cousins stare at the mess. Uncle Leonard stands up, grabs the boy by one ear and drags him to the door. 'You go and cool off outside.'

Alone in the cold hall the boy takes his old jacket down from its hook. The collar smells like cousin Bartholomew. The boy pleads, 'Give me back my strength.' He goes and stands in front of the mirror. 'Fly me home.' But the jacket has lost its power. The cold glass makes him smooth and icy inside.

'You're in love with yourself,' says Aunt Marie when she catches him there on her way through to the kitchen.

No, you old bag! Now that he's staying with such ugly people, he spends a long time looking at himself to find out who he's like. He begs the mirror to make him look different. Browner and more like someone from that other country . . . not sprung from the wet clay. Not bent over under low clouds. He misses the glaring light of the coast, the sand in bed, the dunes . . . it's so almighty flat here, God, how he misses his mountains . . . Mr Java, his Krakatoa on sea.

He creeps to bed, pulls the blankets up over his head. He spends a long time mumbling quietly. There's no answer from God either.

the homecoming

The sea murmurs through the streets of the village. Behind the dune, not far from home, a tractor hums, the new lifeboat-service tractor. They're practising on the loose sand. The sun shines like a diamond. Mother has picked the boy up from the station, she doesn't have many questions or much to say. Mr Java couldn't come. Yes, he's been home for a few days now, in bed . . . still too tired to stand at the window. He's not better yet, but things are going to be better. The girls wait for him in the bicycle hall. Giggling. The hurricane lamps are covered with dust, a spider has cocooned the key to the stable.

When the boy stops at the doorstep to let his mother go first, he stretches his arms out to her. His muscles are tense. He has grown, becoming skinnier and much more manly. He still wants her to give him a kiss and a cuddle, but she can't manage it. She says, 'Your father has missed you terribly.'

Samson behind the curtain

'He's as mad as ever,' says middle sister.

'It started again when that kid came back,' says first sister.

'There's a really scary look in his eyes.' Third sister hardly dares to take Mr Java tea in bed.

'They've both got that lightning in their eyes. Did you see the way that kid squeezed the bread? He kicks and lashes out. He won't listen to reason.' First sister hands out cigarettes, the hall is fuming.

The boy pinches his nose, he mustn't sneeze because otherwise he'd betray his hiding place on the other side of the curtain. But he'd like to tear the cigarettes out of their painted mouths: they are so cheap.

'I'm moving out after the summer,' first sister announces.

Middle sister groans with jealousy. 'We're breaking up,' third sister moans.

'No, we won't let each other go.' The girls comple-
ment each other: 'We're strong.' 'We've proved that.'
'They . . . they drive each other crazy.' 'How long do
you think Horse-Man will last?' 'Poor Mummy.'

The boy tears the curtain aside. There he stands,
powerful, like Samson between the pillars. Proud and
with his legs spread wide. He berates the girls as
godless whores, cursing them in the language of the
Book. They're not having it and storm over, pulling
his curls, trying to get him under control. Blind with
rage, he does what he had first forbidden himself
from doing: he knocks the cigarettes out of their
hands.

the psychiatrist

'As a last exercise we're going to draw your house,' Dr Kofferman says, pulling a stack of white paper out of his drawer. 'How many rooms are there in your house?'

'I don't know.'

'You don't know? And you've lived there your whole life? Let's draw a map together and count them.' Dr Kofferman holds out a big tin box with a rainbow of colours.

After dilly-dallying for a long time, the boy chooses one of four browns – sepia. 'With the cellar, doctor?'

'From the roof to the cellar.'

The boy starts with the view – the dunes at the back and the pines and pasture in front – but at the walls of the house it goes wrong . . . The pencil doesn't want to, it twists in his hand, the point breaks, another shade of brown isn't any better. He changes, scratches, turns it into a maze. The doctor intervenes. 'Start all over again and do it calmly this time.'

The mirror house appears on the page, get rid of it. After the fourth sheet, they manage it together: the wide roof under the dune and beneath it, in clumsy perspective, a plan of squares and rectangles: the bicycle hall, kitchen, cellar and all the rooms, including the neighbours' on the left and at the back.

'So . . . Now we'll give each room a colour,' says Dr Kofferman. 'You choose.' The hall gets grey. Why? That's where the girls smoke. The kitchen, red – blood. The sitting room gets two colours: green for the mushed food on the walls, black for the windows – Mr Java's old post. And Father and Mother's bedroom? Dr Kofferman asks questions and sharpens pencils while the boy adds colours and betrays the life behind their walls.

'What's your favourite spot?' asks Dr Kofferman. The boy shrugs. The doctor points at the black in the sitting room. No. The dark blue in the boy's room. No. 'Has anything nasty ever happened there?' No. 'The bathroom then?' The boiler leaks. 'The girls' room?' A yellow pencil rolls off the table nervously. 'Which room do you like best of all?' In his thoughts the boy wanders through the drawing. 'Where do you feel safe?' The boy doesn't understand what the doctor means. 'The kitchen? Where Mother cooks nice meals? No? Oh. Here maybe . . . Or here?'

Scared. Scared. Scared in every room. The boy takes the red with the sharpest point and scratches the house to shreds. Tears the paper, crumples it up into a ball, kneading it hard in both fists . . .

'What do you mean by that?' the doctor asks.

'I'm the bomb.'

in the bath

She's never seen Mr Java so emaciated and frail, not even in the old days when he had just come through the war. It's not the ribs that shock her or the way he searches for her arm when he wants to stand up, it's his face and, most of all, his eyes and voice . . . They're dull, the sparkle is gone, the excitement, the rage, yes, she misses that too, when he talks, those sharp agitated sounds, the spicy accentuation and all those crisp-fried old-fashioned words, so typical of people who learnt the language of a distant mother country under the equator . . . They're gone, adjusted, blunted . . . He has become estranged from his own tongue.

Every morning Mother leads him to the bath, step by step they walk through the hall together, arm in arm, tile by tile, saying almost nothing to each other − a pat on a hand, two fingers seeking each other . . .

The boy follows them silently, listens as the hook of the bathroom door falls into the eye, climbs up on a stool and looks in through the round hole above the door. He wipes the glass clean, but that's no help, it's misted over on the inside. He sees steam but still he sees Mother helping Mr Java out of his dressing gown and him waiting for her assistance, crooked and trembling, lifting his skinny legs to step into the water, sitting down carefully, groaning. He sees Mother's soaping hands. Neck, back, chest . . . arms up, fingers spread, those brownish–yellow, powerful hands that had so much rage in them . . . She lathers them white. Mother and Mr Java haven't touched each other like this in years, gently and perfumed with bubbles of froth that dance up between them.

And contained in those bubbles are their words, like in a cartoon.

'I've treated you badly,' says Mr Java.

'And I haven't been nice to you,' says Mother.

'I'll do better.'

'You'll get your strength back.'

'But not as angry . . .'

'That's just in you.'

'Scrub it away,' says Mr Java.

The water runs over their words. But the boy hears everything, he sees everything. He too has slow eyes and forgets nothing.